# Our Own Stories

## SECOND EDITION

*Readings for Cross-cultural Communication*

# Our Own Stories

SECOND EDITION

*Readings for Cross-cultural Communication*

*Norine Dresser*

Longman

**Our Own Stories: Readings for Cross-cultural Communication, Second Edition**

Pearson Education, 10 Bank Street, White Plains, NY 10606

Editorial director: Joanne Dresner
Senior development editor: Debbie Sistino
Acquisitions editor: Allen Ascher
Development editor: Randee Falk
Assistant editor: Jessica Miller
Production editor: Elizabeth Pleva
Text design: Jack Schwartz
Cover design: Joseph DePinho
Cover photo: Provided by Guidance Associates
Text art: Karen Henrickson Sothoron

Library of Congress Cataloging-in-Publication Data
Our own stories: Readings for cross-cultural communication /
    [compiled by] Norine Dresser. -- 2nd ed.
        p.    cm.
        ISBN 0-201-84670-5
        1. English language--Textbooks for foreign speakers.
    2. Intercultural communication--Problems, exercises, etc.    3. United
    States--Civilization--Problems, exercises, etc.    4. College prose,
    American--California--Los Angeles.    5. Culture--Problems, exercises,
    etc.    6. American essays--Minority authors.    7. Readers--United
    States.        I. Dresser, Norine.
    PE1128.097    1995
    428.6'4--dc20                                          95-21738
                                                              CIP

8 9 10 11 12 13 14 15-CRS-05 04 03 02 01 00

# DEDICATION

*In loving memory of my father, Issidore Shapiro,*
*who understood the power of a tale well told.*

# CONTENTS

# INTRODUCTION

*Our Own Stories* is based upon cross-cultural communication misunderstandings described in essays written by students at California State University, Los Angeles. Most of these students were born in Asia and Latin America, yet regardless of their origin their stories are universal—the theme of the outsider trying to become part of a new culture. The students wrote about their astounding experiences in response to the following assignment: "Describe a time when cultural differences caused a problem for you in this country." The resulting essays—sad, funny, and inspiring—are the backbone of this book and the centerpiece of each unit. Written from the heart, they demonstrate that the road to becoming a new American is filled with many bumps and wrong turns. Therefore, these stories give encouragement to other ESL students by showing that every newcomer makes mistakes. In addition, the tales point to the problem areas in understanding American culture, which usually center around customs, beliefs, and values. Further, the stories reveal that it is advantageous to be familiar with the customs of the many different groups of people who live here.

*Our Own Stories* is designed for intermediate ESL students to improve their conversation and reading skills as well as provide information about American culture. There are twenty units and each one begins with a real student's dilemma caused by cultural differences. Each unit deals with one particular custom—for example, food taboos. Although it is not mandatory that the units be followed in sequence, please note that the earlier part of the book deals with simpler cultural issues, while those essays toward the back relate to more complex and sophisticated subjects.

Within each unit are diversified activities to develop discussion about the topic and to build English-language skills through exercises such as comprehension and inference questions, vocabulary development, interviews, and oral and written reports.

Activities have been designed to be as self-explanatory as possible and flexibility has been allowed for. For example, teachers may select one unit and use it over more than one class meeting, or if there are time limitations, they may skip some of the later activities within the unit—for instance, Follow-Up. However, to get the maximum from each unit, it is recommended that all sections (described below) be used.

## Do You Know . . . ?

The questions and accompanying illustration in this section are designed to focus the students' attention on the topic and to anticipate where the cultural conflict might lie. Through discussion, teachers and students become aware of what they already know about the particular cultural issue.

## The Story

Reading the story twice is a good way to ensure understanding. One method is to have students first read to themselves. The second time they can take turns reading aloud one line at a time. In this way it becomes apparent where students are having problems with pronunciation. If they stumble, this may also be a signal that they are unfamiliar with the vocabulary.

## Comprehension

Five sets of questions follow each story. Each set adds a new level of complexity. Section A requires true/false responses to confirm basic understanding of the content, while Section B asks students to give answers in phrases or sentences. Section C calls for opinions. This empowers students by teaching that their opinions are valuable. In many parts of the world, student opinions are never asked for. However, since having an opinion and drawing inferences are valued in American education, students need practice in this—particularly if they plan to go on to higher education. Section D challenges students further by asking them to add new ideas and details to the story. To do so, they must focus on character analysis and understand human motivation. These are necessary tools for interpreting literature *and* life. Section E entails a comparison of what the main character learned and what students learned from the story. First, readers must synthesize the plot to grasp the point of the story. Then they must make comparisons between themselves and the protagonists. While at first glance one might expect that the main characters learn the same lessons as the readers, this is not necessarily so. Asking what students learned from the story spurs them to formulate ideas at higher levels of abstraction.

## Vocabulary

Acquiring vocabulary consists of more than memorizing a laundry list of words. To avoid rote learning, five varieties of vocabulary exercises aim at having students understand new words and concepts through story context. While the exercises vary in complexity, all endeavor to have students ultimately incorporate the words into their everyday lexicon. In addition, an assortment of approaches ensures continued student interest. In some instances, words that cannot be deciphered from context have been defined in the margin.

## CULTURE CAPSULE

This section contains information about American cultural rules. Students can read to themselves or to each other, or if preferred, the teacher may want to read aloud to the class and then ask questions to ensure comprehension.

## Cultural  Exchange

This activity focuses on similarities and differences in cultures. Having students describe their own cultural customs fosters pride in their own heritage. At the same time, they are learning about their classmates' backgrounds, which may be similar to or distinct from their own. This presents a perfect opportunity for helping students develop respect for one another's culture. One way to do this is by avoiding judgmental words like "strange" or "weird," which some students might want to use in evaluating their classmates' traditions. Teachers might point out that it is difficult to be objective about another culture without complete information about the values and customs of that culture.

## Expansion

The focus of Expansion is on the rules and customs of American culture through activities that improve vocabulary skills. Students may be asked to complete a crossword puzzle or a word search, conduct a survey, or participate in decision-making activities. Answers to the puzzles appear at the back of the book.

# Follow-Up ✓

The first activity requires students to prepare either a written or oral report. Not only does this bring closure to the unit, but it also sharpens skills that will move the student toward the next level of language proficiency.

The second follow-up can be done in class, time permitting, or can be used as an extra-credit, take-home assignment. These activities are quite varied throughout the book.

Finally, I would like to know how ESL classes enjoy this book. If teachers or students have any suggestions or comments, I would be pleased to hear from them. If teachers use the same writing assignment that was the basis of *Our Own Stories* ("Describe a time when cultural differences caused a problem for you in this country."), and they have responses they would like to share, or if students would like to send me their own responses to this topic, I would appreciate receiving them. Please write to me at the following address:

Norine Dresser
c/o Addison-Wesley/Longman
World Language Division
10 Bank Street
White Plains, NY 10606-1951

# ACKNOWLEDGMENTS

Every book begins as an Aha!, and the inspiration for *Our Own Stories* occurred when I read sixty student essays on the topic of cultural differences. Charmed, I discussed the possibilities of collecting more examples to create a book and received excellent feedback and assistance from my colleagues at California State University, Los Angeles, and those who teach elsewhere. I am grateful to all of them: Nancy Allison, David Beaulieu, Lise Buranen, Mike Cappella, Rosella Cappella, Virginia Crane, Chloe Diepenbrock, Sally Gardner (and her great ACLP teachers), Karen Gregg, Bill Hart, Jayasri Hart, Nancy Hutcheon, Elliott Oring, Michael Pessah, Morris Polan, Buddy Roberts, Arpi Sarafian, Sharon Smartt, and Nick Zonen.

In addition, I was indeed fortunate to have met Joanne Dresner, Editorial Director of ESL at Addison-Wesley/Longman, who immediately recognized the possibilities in my embryonic idea, gave me encouragement, and eventually—the green light. I toast her vision and all her kindness. Further, I would like to express appreciation to Debbie Sistino, Senior Development Editor, who worked closely with me. Her guidance was always sensitive, clear-cut, and reassuring. I also thank Randee "Hawkeye" Falk for all her "right-on" suggestions and fine-tuned editing.

To my consortium of gifted friends upon whom I selfishly rely for consultation on all projects—Kay Enell, Montserrat Fontes, Janice Garey, and Jan Steward—I say, "Thanks, buddies, I couldn't have done it without your help!"

Of course, this book could never have come to fruition without the support of my husband, Harold, who endured my complaints and grouchiness, yet lovingly made rush trips to the post office and stationery supply store and brought in all those great take-out dinners.

Finally, one of my fondest memories is when, as an elementary-school girl, I helped my two European-born grandmothers with writing assignments from their adult-school English classes. I relished the position of child being teacher to grown-ups. Today, as a grandmother myself, I still feel the same pleasure, this time in helping young students learn English. Thus, it is to the memory of my first students, grandmothers Anna Friesh and Ida Shapiro, and my wonderful CSULA composition students that this book is dedicated. I pay tribute to the hundreds who shared their delightful stories with me and, in particular, those student authors whose adventures were selected for inclusion here. I offer you my heartfelt gratitude.

**Student Authors**

Juan Carlos Cardenas
Norma Garcia
John C. Gomez, Jr.
Janice Nghi Nha Ha
Raymond Kwong
Tuan Lam
Yuxue Li
Le My Lien
Monica Martinez
Chieng Pe

Chau Phu
Rosa A. Rodriguez-Cabral
Kin Tchang
Hoa T. Van
Norma A. Velasco
Yung Ho Wang
Pat Wong
Lynn Cheng-Ping Yang
Tony Yang
Catherine Yee

# UNIT 1
# *Clothing*

## ? Do you know…

1. What do most Americans wear to school?
2. What do teachers wear?

# The Dress of Lace

*Read the story.*

My name is Linh. I'm an eighteen-year-old girl. My ethnic background and native language are Vietnamese. This is a story about what happened to me on my first day of school in America. I was nine years old.

A few weeks before school started, my aunt, my uncle, and some of my dad's friends came to visit us and they brought a lot of presents. I was surprised when I found clothing in one of the boxes. The clothes were nice but ordinary. They weren't special or fancy except for one dress. It was a dress of lace. There was lace surrounding the neck and the sleeves and lace on the bottom. I was very happy when I saw this dress.

On the first day of school I wanted to look my best and impress the other students. I wanted them to make friends with me, so I put on my fancy dress of lace. But when I got to school, all the students stared at me. They were laughing and saying something in English. I didn't know why they were doing this. I thought that maybe they had never seen an Asian girl in a dress before or that they wanted to make friends with me but were embarrassed to come over.

In the classroom an American teacher spoke English to me and pointed at my dress, but I didn't know what she was saying so I just smiled. The whole morning she didn't let me walk around or stand up. I had to sit all the way in the last row in the back of the room. During lunch, when all the other students had gone, an Asian teacher came into the room. The minute she saw me she spoke to me in Vietnamese. She told me that I shouldn't wear a nightgown to school, that in America people only wear nightgowns to sleep in! I was so embarrassed that I almost burst into tears. That morning when I left home, I thought I looked good, but I didn't. Instead, I embarrassed myself on my first day of school. I felt like not going to school anymore.

This embarrassment taught me not to try to impress others or I might end up making a fool out of myself. I also learned the difference between a fancy dress and a nightgown!

**lace**—A cloth that is made of fine threads and looks like net

**nightgown**—A piece of women's clothing, like a loose dress to sleep in

**fool**—A person who acts unwisely

# Comprehension

*A. Tell whether these sentences are true or false.*

1. Linh came to the United States when she was eighteen years old.

2. Linh and her parents have other relatives in the United States.

3. Linh wore her dress of lace in a store.

4. Linh wore her dress of lace on the first day of school.

5. Linh's schoolmates were surprised when they saw her because they had never seen an Asian girl in a dress before.

6. The American teacher put Linh in the back of the classroom.

7. As soon as the American teacher explained the problem, Linh understood.

8. Linh did not enjoy her first day of school.

*B. Answer these questions.*

1. How did Linh get her dress of lace?

2. Why did Linh want to wear the dress of lace to school?

3. What did Linh's schoolmates do when they saw her?

4. What did the American teacher have Linh do? Why?

5. When did Linh find out she was wearing a nightgown?

6. How did Linh feel when she found out she was wearing a nightgown?

*C. Give your opinion.*

1. Do you think Linh's classmates behaved badly toward her?

2. What do you think Linh's teacher should have done?

3. Linh says she learned that she should not try to impress others. Do you agree with Linh's conclusion? Why or why not?

4. What kind of clothes would you wear on your first day of school or work? Explain your choice.

5. Suppose you were going someplace and you did not know what would be appropriate to wear. What would you do?

**D.** *Now add your own ideas to the story.*

1. What did some of the students say to each other about Linh in her nightgown?

2. What did the teacher think about Linh? Did she like her or dislike her? Did she think Linh was smart or stupid? Did she feel sorry for Linh?

3. What did Linh's mother say to her when she came home so upset?

4. How did Linh feel when she returned to school the next day?

5. How did the students treat Linh when she returned the next day?

**E.** *Compare yourself with Linh.*

1. What did Linh learn?

2. What did you learn from Linh's story?

# Vocabulary ▐▐▐▐➡

*Complete the sentences with the appropriate words. Circle the letter of the correct answer.*

1. When Linh described her <u>ethnic background</u> she was referring to _____.
   a. part of a picture or painting
   b. the cultural group to which she belonged

2. If Linh's <u>native language</u> is Vietnamese, that means _____.
   a. it is the language she first learned as a child
   b. it is a language she learned later on in life

3. When Linh found <u>ordinary</u> clothes in the box she was describing something _____.
   a. unusual
   b. usual

4. Linh's <u>fancy</u> dress was _____.
   a. plain
   b. elegant

5. If Linh's dress had <u>lace</u> on it, that means it was _____.
   a. probably pretty
   b. probably not pretty

6. When Linh wanted to <u>impress</u> the other students, that meant _____.
   a. she cared what they thought about her
   b. she didn't care what they thought about her

7. When Linh felt <u>embarrassed</u>, she felt _____.
   a. happy
   b. unhappy

8. Linh was worried about making a <u>fool</u> of herself. That means she feared that _____.
   a. others would have respect for her
   b. others would have no respect for her

9. When the teacher <u>pointed</u> to Linh's dress, she was _____.
   a. using her finger to direct attention to the dress
   b. drawing a picture of the dress

10. Linh wanted to <u>make friends</u> with the students. She wanted them _____.
    a. to like her
    b. to like someone else but not her

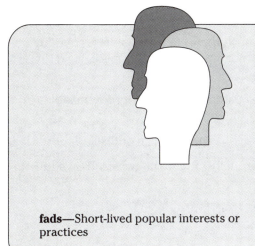

# CULTURE CAPSULE

Students usually wear casual, not formal, clothes to school. Jeans, T-shirts, and sneakers are popular among both girls and boys. It is also acceptable to dress up more. Students dress according to their personal preferences and sometimes are influenced by fads, or the latest fashions.

In some private schools and religious schools, students wear uniforms. Although public schools do not use uniforms, they sometimes have "dress codes," or rules about what clothes may *not* be worn to school.

**fads**—Short-lived popular interests or practices

# Cultural Exchange

**A.** *Tell whether these sentences about the United States are true or false.*

1. Students wear uniforms to public schools.

2. There are no rules, and students can wear whatever they want.

3. Wearing a nightgown to school is acceptable.

4. Students cannot wear sneakers to school.

5. Students are not allowed to wear the latest fashion clothing to school.

**B.** *Answer these questions about your country in writing or aloud.*
What kinds of clothing do you usually wear when you go to . . .

1. School?

2. Work?

3. The market?

4. A restaurant?

5. The movies?

6. Bed?

**C.** *Discuss these questions with your classmates.*

1. What clothing would you wear indoors in your country, but never outside in public?

2. Is there any clothing from your country that you would not wear in public if you visited the United States?

3. From what you know about American clothing customs, is there anything you would not wear because you do not like it or because it is against the clothing customs of your country?

4. In what ways are American clothing customs similar to clothing customs in your country? In what ways are they different?

5. What American clothing customs do you especially like or dislike?

6. Do American students dress more formally or more informally than students in your country?

7. Did anything surprise you about this story?

# Expansion

*To increase your vocabulary about clothing, solve this crossword puzzle with words from the list below.*

bikini          necktie          shoes          sweatsuit

bracelets       nightgown        sneakers       tuxedo

hat             purses           suit

jacket          sandals          sunglasses

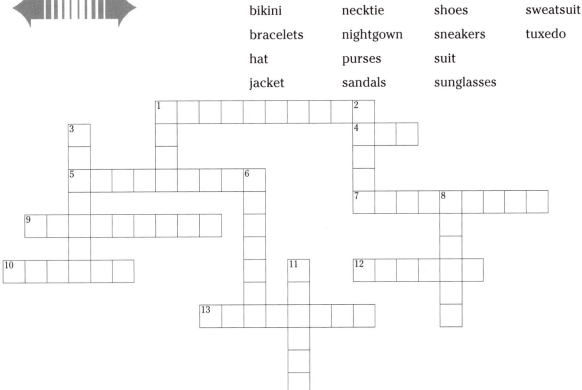

## Across

1. Good for the beach but not for the office
4. Good for outdoors but not for indoors
5. Good for sleeping but not for school
7. Good for exercising but not for a wedding
9. A person can wear many of these at the same time
10. Most women carry these, and some wear them on belts around their waists
12. Good for the winter but not for the summer
13. Good for the gym but not for church

## Down

1. Good for job interviews
2. Some people wear them indoors; others take them off
3. Good for the summer but not for the winter
6. Good for a business meeting but not necessary for school
8. Good for a wedding but not for work
11. Good for the beach but not to go shopping

**tuxedo**—A man's formal evening suit, usually black

# Follow-Up ✓

**A.** *Give a brief oral or written report. Choose number 1 or 2.*

1. Tell about a special occasion when you were either underdressed or overdressed.

2. Tell about a time when you tried to impress someone by your appearance but it did not work out as expected.

*When you describe the event, consider including some of the following details:*

When did this happen? Where did it take place?

Why did the event occur?

What happened? What went wrong?

How did you feel? How did others feel?

What did you learn from this experience?

**B.** *A friend from your native country is planning a two-week visit to the United States. He or she can bring only one suitcase. In a letter, tell your friend what clothing he or she* should *and* should not *pack.*

# U N I T 2
# *Holidays*

## ? Do you know...

**1.** How do children celebrate Halloween?

**2.** What are three other American holidays?

# Trick or Treat?

*Read the story.*

Hi. My name is Tony, and I remember the first Halloween I spent in the United States. I was in the sixth grade, trying my best to study as hard as I could to overcome the language barrier. Even though I studied English in my native country, Hong Kong, I was still not able to communicate in English. I realized that my classmates were talking about how they would dress on Halloween, but I didn't know what Halloween was.

That year Halloween came on Saturday. I was home most of the day studying. I didn't have a chance to go outside and see how everyone was dressed, because if I had, the following incident would not have happened.

After dinner, my parents turned off all the lights and went to their room. They did this so they could ignore the children coming to the house for treats. But they didn't tell me about it. I was in my room, so I didn't know what was happening. After a while I went out of my room to get a drink of water. I realized that the house was dark very early, and I thought that my parents were tired after a long day of work. I didn't have any brothers or sisters to come with me, so I felt very much alone in the dark house. I was not used to that. Then it happened. When I was drinking my glass of water, the doorbell rang. I looked out my window. There, standing at my front door, were four or five ghosts accompanied by a witch!

I was so scared that I started screaming and I covered myself with my blanket. I tried not to scream, but I couldn't stop. My father came running into my room asking me what was the matter. I told him about the ghosts and the witch, and he explained to me about Halloween. I was relieved after realizing the truth but I also felt embarrassed about being afraid.

That was my first experience with Halloween. Now, each year I remind my parents, weeks before Halloween, to buy candy, and when I do, my dad laughs at me about that incident.

**barrier**—Something that prevents progress

**ignore**—To take no notice of; to disregard

**ghost**—A dead spirit who returns to earth

**witch**—A woman who has magic powers

# Comprehension

**A.** *Tell whether these sentences are true or false.*

1. At school Tony did not understand Halloween.

2. That year Halloween took place on a school day.

3. On Halloween, children wear their regular school clothes.

4. Tony had brothers and sisters living with him.

5. On Halloween night Tony was home alone.

6. At first Tony thought there were real ghosts and a real witch at his door.

7. Tony's parents did not understand American Halloween customs.

8. Now Tony reminds his parents to have treats ready for Halloween.

**B.** *Answer these questions.*

1. On Halloween day why didn't Tony notice people in their costumes?

2. On Halloween night why were the lights turned off in Tony's house?

3. Why did Tony leave his bedroom?

4. What did Tony see and do when he looked out the window?

5. How did Tony feel after his father told him about Halloween?

**C.** *Give your opinion.*

1. Why do you think Tony's parents didn't want the children to come to their house?

2. Why do you think the parents didn't explain the holiday to their son?

3. Why do you think Tony didn't want to scream, even though he was frightened?

4. How do you think Tony's father felt when he saw his son was so frightened?

5. Do you think Tony should be angry with his parents for not telling him about Halloween? Why or why not?

**D.** *Now add your own ideas to the story.*

1. What does Tony think the ghosts and witch are going to do to him?

2. When Tony screams, what does his father think has happened?

3. Do you think Tony will lose respect for himself over this incident? Or will he lose respect for his father?

**E.** *Compare yourself with Tony.*

1. What did Tony learn?

2. What did you learn from Tony's story?

---

# Vocabulary

*Complete the sentences with the appropriate words. Circle the letter of the correct answer.*

1. Tony writes about the <u>language barrier</u>. He is referring to _____.
   a. communication difficulties due to language differences
   b. a roadblock on his street

2. When Tony wants to <u>overcome</u> the language barrier, he wishes _____.
   a. to have someone come over to his house
   b. to improve his communication in another language

3. Tony's <u>incident</u> _____.
   a. is the story of what happened to him
   b. is an accident

4. Tony's parents wanted to <u>ignore</u> the children. They wanted to _____.
   a. not pay attention to them
   b. pay attention to them

5. <u>Halloween</u> is a holiday where _____.
   a. children dress in costumes and go door-to-door saying, "Trick-or-treat"
   b. children dye hard-boiled eggs bright colors

6. Halloween <u>treats</u> are usually _____.
   a. candy
   b. songs the children sing

## CULTURE CAPSULE

On Halloween, which comes on October 31, children go "trick-or-treating." The children dress up in costumes, often pretending to be something scary, like ghosts and witches. They then go from house to house asking for candy or other treats. If they do not receive any, they might threaten to play tricks—like overturning trash cans or spraying windows with shaving cream. But most children do not really play tricks.

At Halloween time, you will see many jack-o'-lanterns. These are pumpkins that have been cut to look like human faces and often have a candle inside.

# Cultural Exchange

*A. Tell whether these sentences about the United States are true or false.*

1. Halloween comes on November 30.

2. Turning over trash cans is an example of a trick.

3. A jack-o'-lantern is made out of a pumpkin.

4. "Trick-or-treating" is something that children do on this holiday.

5. Ghosts and witches are not scary.

*B. Answer these questions about your culture in writing or aloud.*

1. What kind of holiday do you celebrate that deals with ghosts?

2. What kind of holiday do you celebrate where people dress up in costumes?

3. What kind of holiday do you have that celebrates an important religious event?

4. What kind of holiday do you have that celebrates an important historic event?

5. What kind of holiday do you have that celebrates a particular family member (Mother's Day, Father's Day, Grandparents' Day, other)?

6. What kind of holiday do you have that celebrates the beginning of a new season (spring, summer, fall, winter)?

*C. Discuss these questions with your classmates.*

1. Do you think you would enjoy celebrating Halloween?

2. What holiday custom from the United States or another culture would you like to celebrate?

3. How do you celebrate birthdays?

4. For which holidays do you send greeting cards?

5. Have you ever introduced one of your own holiday customs to someone from another culture?

# Expansion

Christmas

New Year's Eve

Thanksgiving

Saint Patrick's Day

April Fools' Day

Easter

Halloween

Memorial Day

Fourth of July

Valentine's Day

*Draw a line from the name of the holiday listed in the left-hand column to the appropriate description in the right-hand column.*

Day to wear green; especially important for the Irish

Baby rabbits, colored eggs, family dinners, new clothes

Exchange gifts; fat old man with long white beard and red suit

Day to honor soldiers killed in battle; parades and visits to cemeteries

Children in costume go door-to-door asking for treats

People play harmless tricks on one another

Loud noises at midnight; parties, dancing

Day for love and for lovers; people give cards, candies, and flowers to those they love

Family gatherings, turkey dinners; Pilgrims and Indians long ago

Fireworks; picnics and barbecues

# Follow-Up ✓

**A.** *Give a brief oral or written report. Tell about a holiday that you celebrate and enjoy. When you describe the holiday, consider including some of the following details:*

What is the name of the holiday?

When does it take place?

What is the reason for this holiday? (religious? seasonal? historic? etc.)

What are some of the activities that people do on this holiday?

**B.** *Choose one of the celebration categories below and think of a holiday from your country that belongs to that category.*

| New Year | spring | harvest |
| winter | historic | religious |

1. Now play five-card draw. Take five 3 × 5 index cards and draw pictures that give information about the holiday. On each card you will show certain information. If you have no information about one of the categories, leave out that card.

**Information**

Card 1:  What is the name of the celebration? When is it observed? What is it about?

Card 2:  Show what activities (games, rituals, etc.) there are.

Card 3:  Show what foods are prepared and eaten.

Card 4:  Show what clothing is worn.

Card 5:  Show who the participants are.

Even if you are not a good artist, make each card as exciting as possible. Use markers, crayons, colored pens, or paste on pictures cut from magazines.

2. After you have completed the five cards, put them up on a large wall or board under the appropriate celebration heading. Compare your cards with your classmates' cards.

# UNIT 3
# *Health and Illness*

## ? Do you know...

1. What kinds of medicines do you take if you get sick with a cold or the flu?

2. Do you know anyone who has been healed by someone who was not a doctor or a nurse?

# Coining

*Read the story.*

My father was born in China, and my mother was born in Cambodia. They adopted the traditional values of their cultures and passed these values on to me. I was also born in Cambodia, but my family and I have been living in the United States for about ten years now. I have even chosen an American name and call myself Wendy.

There were not many Asian students where I first went to school, so when I got sick I didn't know what to do, whether to stay home or go to school. One day when I got home I didn't feel well. My mother felt my forehead and noticed that I had a fever. She said, "I'd better coin you to get rid of the bad pressure so you can go to school tomorrow."

Coining is a Cambodian tradition we use to help us feel better when we are sick. A coin is dipped in oil and then its edge is rubbed against the sick person's chest, back, and neck. Coining hurts. This time it hurt so much that my mother had to put her leg on my back so I would stay still. In the end, I felt better inside, but outside I hurt because of the red lines that appeared from the coining.

The next day in class when I went up to ask my teacher about my workbook, she noticed the red marks on my neck and asked me what happened. I tried to explain to her with body language because I couldn't speak well yet. She called someone to take me to the nurse to be examined. The nurse had never seen anything like this before. The principal and the nurse showed me all kinds of objects they thought my parents used to punish me. They thought I was the victim of child abuse. I tried to show them what happened by taking a coin and rubbing it against my arm. They still didn't understand because each red mark was the size of a ruler in width and the marks were deep red like bruises.

The school didn't have an Asian translator. I had never been in a situation like this, and I was afraid of what the people at school would do to me. But they let

**values**—People's ideas about the worth of certain qualities, such as honesty, hard work, education, respect

**get rid of**—To make something go away

**child abuse**—Mistreatment of a child either by beating or by neglect

**bruises**—Discolored sore places on the skin

me call home and I told my parents what happened. Since my parents couldn't speak English, the school called a church agency, which found a Mandarin translator for us.

The translator and my dad went to the school. The people at the school office had angry faces. All my dad could do was explain in detail that coining is a part of our tradition and that we were newcomers. The principal was going to report it to the police, but when he finally understood better what had happened, he dropped the case. He advised my parents not to do coining again. He said that next time I was sick I should stay home and go to a doctor for medicine.

# Comprehension

**A.** *Tell whether these sentences are true or false.*

1. Wendy's mother wanted Wendy to stay home when she was sick.

2. Coining is a form of gambling.

3. Coining hurts.

4. Coining leaves red marks and bruises on the body.

5. The school nurse was familiar with coining.

6. The principal and nurse thought Wendy was a victim of child abuse.

7. Wendy's father and a translator explained coining to the principal.

8. The principal told the parents not to do coining again.

**B.** *Answer these questions.*

1. Why did Wendy's mother use coining?

2. Why did Wendy's mother put her leg on Wendy's back?

3. How is coining done?

4. Why did the principal want to call the police?

5. If Wendy ever gets sick again, what does the principal want her to do?

**C.** *Give your opinion.*

1. Why didn't Wendy know whether to stay home or go to school when she was sick?

2. Why did Wendy's mother use coining instead of taking her to a doctor?

3. Why would Wendy agree to the coining even though she knew it hurt and caused red marks?

4. Did the teacher handle this situation in the best way? What else could she have done?

5. Do you think Wendy's family should give up coining just because the principal told them to? Why or why not?

**D.** *Now add your own ideas to the story.*

1. How does Wendy feel about the principal? Is she angry with him, or embarrassed? Does he make her feel afraid?

2. Is her father confused, angry, or embarrassed?

3. Does her father feel guilty even though he and his wife weren't trying to harm their daughter?

4. How does Wendy's father feel about the school interfering with their home health treatment for their child?

5. Does the principal believe that coining caused the bruises, or does he still suspect the parents have harmed their daughter?

**E.** *Compare yourself with Wendy.*

1. What did Wendy learn from this experience?

2. What did you learn from Wendy's story?

# Vocabulary ▐▐▐▐▶

*Complete the sentences with one of the following words or phrases.*

| traditional values | principal | punished | child abuse |
|---|---|---|---|
| advised | marks | fever | objects |

1. The teacher, the principal, and the nurse all thought Wendy was a victim of _____.

2. The person in charge of Wendy's school is called the _____.

3. Wendy's forehead felt hot, so her mother knew that Wendy had a _____.

4. Respecting and obeying parents and honoring older persons are examples of _____.

5. _____ can be sticks, chairs, pencils, shoes, newspapers.

6. If you rub hard against someone's skin, it will leave red _____.

7. When they saw the red lines on Wendy's body, the school staff thought that Wendy's father had _____ her too hard.

8. The school _____ Wendy's parents not to use coining again.

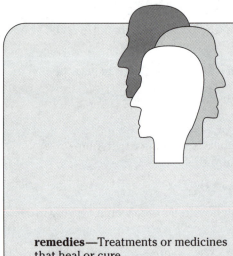

# CULTURE CAPSULE

For certain illnesses like colds and flus, Americans often try home remedies, that is, methods of getting better that do not involve a doctor or medicines. For example, a person might stay in bed, have lots of soup and other liquids, use hot steam to make the air moist, and take lots of vitamin C. Americans also buy over-the-counter medicines like aspirin and cough syrup. Over-the-counter medicines are medicines that do not require a prescription, or signed order from a doctor.

For most illnesses, though, Americans go to doctors, who examine them and often write out prescriptions. Home remedies are less common in the United States than in many other parts of the world.

**remedies**—Treatments or medicines that heal or cure

**moist**—Slightly wet or damp

# Cultural Exchange

**A.** *Tell whether these sentences about the United States are true or false.*

1. Americans don't use home remedies.

2. You need a prescription for over-the-counter medicines.

3. Vitamin C is popular for colds and flu.

4. A prescription is an order for medicine that is signed by a doctor.

5. Most Americans avoid aspirin and cough syrup.

***B.*** *Fill in the chart below, and then share your answers with your classmates.*

| In Your Culture, What Kinds of Treatments or Medicine Are Used for the Following: | |
| --- | --- |
| Fever? | |
| Cough? | |
| Diarrhea? | |
| Rash? | |
| Back pain? | |
| Toothache? | |
| Headache? | |
| Burns? | |
| Childbirth? | |
| A screaming infant? | |

***C.*** *Discuss these questions with your classmates.*

1. Do you have anything in your culture that is similar to coining? What do you call it? Describe how it is done.

2. What plants or foods do you use to help you get well or keep you from getting sick?

3. Do you or others you know wear anything around necks, wrists, or waists to keep from getting sick? Describe.

4. In your country, how sick must children be before they can stay home from school?

5. Besides regular doctors and the use of modern medicines, describe other kinds of healers that are used in your culture, such as people who pray, chant, or perform rituals on behalf of a sick person. Have you ever used any of these healers? Describe.

# Expansion

*To increase your vocabulary about medical specialists, solve this crossword puzzle with words from the list below.*

cardiologist     ophthalmologist     radiologist

dentist     orthopedist     surgeon

dermatologist     pediatrician     urologist

neurologist     psychiatrist     obstetrician

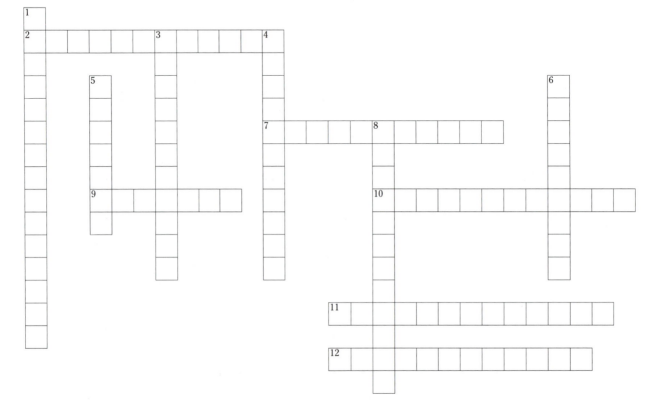

**Across**

2. If your baby is sick, call a(n) . . .
7. If you break your arm
9. If you have to have your appendix removed
10. If you have a heart attack
11. If you have a rash
12. If you're going to have a baby

**Down**

1. If you are having trouble seeing, call a(n) . . .
3. If you need X-rays
4. If you have headaches
5. If you have a toothache
6. If you have trouble urinating
8. If you have emotional problems

# Follow-Up

**A.** *Give a brief oral or written report. Choose number 1 or 2.*

1. Tell about a time when you first tried a different healing method and were surprised by the results.

2. Tell about a time when you disagreed with a doctor or other kind of healer.

*If you choose number 1, consider including some of the following details:*

What was your physical problem? How did this problem come about? When did this happen? Where were you living at the time?

What was the old method you used? What was the new method? Who introduced this new idea to you?

What did you expect to happen? What happened? Why were you surprised?

Did you or would you ever try the method again? Why or why not?

*If you choose number 2, consider including some of the following details:*

What was your physical problem? How did this problem come about?

When did this happen? Where were you living at the time?

What did the doctor or healer want you to do?

Why did you disagree with this? Were you right to disagree? Why?

What was the response of the doctor or healer? Would you go back to him or her again? Why or why not? What did you learn from this?

**B.** *Pick a partner for library research. Then choose and research one of the following topics. Each is a healing method that most doctors* do not *use. Prepare a report for the rest of the class.*

| | |
|---|---|
| acupuncture | homeopathy |
| biofeedback | hypnosis |
| chiropractic | massage |
| faith healing | midwifery |

*In your report consider including some of the following details:*

What kinds of problems is this method used for? How does it work?

Do many people accept this method? Is there any criticism of it?

Who developed this method?

Do you have anything similar in your culture?

Would you ever consider using this method?

# UNIT 4

## *Food Taboos*

**?** ## Do you know...

1. Are there any foods Americans do not eat?

2. Has anyone ever refused to eat food you offered them?

# Hamburgers

*Read the story.*

I am Rafael, a second-generation American of Hispanic descent. I was born in Los Angeles and have lived there for eighteen years. My neighborhood is largely Hispanic. Being raised in a community that has one main ethnic group is both good and bad. It is good because I appreciate my culture. It is bad because I am ignorant of other cultures that inhabit the earth. So, not surprisingly, there was an incident when I experienced culture shock. It happened just recently in the home of Gopal, a friend from India.

One rainy day Gopal, who I have known for five months, invited me to his home. On my way there I stopped and bought hamburgers for him and me. However, I did not tell him about the hamburgers.

Gopal's family was eating in the dining room. Gopal and I were in the living room. I asked him, "Do you mind if I eat some food I bought for us?"

"Go right ahead," he answered. "Here, let's go into the dining room. I'll set a place for you at the table."

I seated myself at the table. Slowly I placed the bag on the table and extracted one hamburger for myself and handed the other one to Gopal. As I sank my teeth into the hamburger, his family abruptly stopped eating their meal and began to stare at me. I asked, "Enjoying your meal?"

Not one person answered me. Their stares and the silence that accompanied the stares sent chills through my body. I was confused.

Finally, after about two minutes, Gopal's mother spoke. She said, "You do not know very much about India and our culture. Did you know that in India the cow is considered sacred? It is sacred because the Hindu religion made it holy. We don't and can't eat beef."

She and the family understood that I did not know about Hinduism. I listened and learned more about India. My interest was undivided and her information was rewarding. As a result of this incident I now think before buying beef products. I keep in mind that other

**taboo**—Something that is forbidden

**descent**—Family origin

**ethnic**—Cultural, religious, national, or racial group

**chills**—Unpleasant coldness

**sacred**—Associated with or dedicated to God or a god

cultures have beliefs that we don't have. I do not think the family, especially Gopal, was affected by the incident. No one was angry at me. It is ironic that Gopal is presently working at Tommy's Burgers.

**ironic**—Unexpected or opposite of what is expected

# Comprehension

**A.** *Tell whether these sentences are true or false.*

1. Rafael was born in Mexico.

2. Gopal was born in India.

3. Rafael and Gopal had been friends since elementary school.

4. Rafael brought hamburgers for himself and Gopal.

5. Gopal's family was offended because of the way Rafael chewed his hamburger.

6. Gopal's mother yelled at Rafael.

7. Rafael was not interested in what Gopal's mother told him.

**B.** *Answer these questions.*

1. What does Rafael consider bad about living in a community composed of mainly one ethnic group?

2. Why was Gopal's family offended by the hamburgers?

3. How did they react?

4. Why don't Hindus eat beef?

5. How did Rafael accept this information?

6. What kind of job does Gopal now have?

**C.** *Give your opinion.*

1. How would you describe Rafael's personality and character?

2. Do you think Gopal's mother handled the situation well? Why or why not?

3. Do you think Rafael handled the situation well? Why or why not?

4. What do you think Rafael gained from this experience?

5. If it is taboo for Hindus to eat beef, how do you explain Gopal working at Tommy's Burgers?

**D.** *Now add your own ideas to the story.*

1. How does Rafael feel when Gopal's family stares at him? Is he surprised or embarrassed, or does he feel some other way?

2. Is Rafael apologetic after he learns that he has offended Gopal's family? Does he feel guilty?

3. How does Gopal's mother feel about Rafael? Is she annoyed or is she sympathetic with his lack of understanding?

4. Does Gopal's mother educate or embarrass Rafael?

5. After this experience will Rafael visit Gopal's home again? Will his relationship with Gopal remain the same?

**E.** *Compare yourself with Rafael.*

1. What did Rafael learn?

2. What did you learn from Rafael's story?

# Vocabulary |||➡

*Complete the sentences with one of the following words or phrases.*

| | | | |
|---|---|---|---|
| neighborhood | chills | culture shock | sacred |
| rewarding | ignorant | extracted | Hindu religion |

1. When Rafael learned some unexpected information about Gopal's family, he experienced _____ .

2. Rafael felt _____ in his body when the family stopped eating and talking to stare at him.

3. Rafael lived in a _____ where most people were Hispanic.

4. For many people in India, cows are _____ .

5. Rafael _____ hamburgers from the bag.

6. Gopal's family were members of the _____ .

7. Rafael admitted that he was _____ about other cultures.

8. Rafael believed he learned something _____ from Gopal's mother.

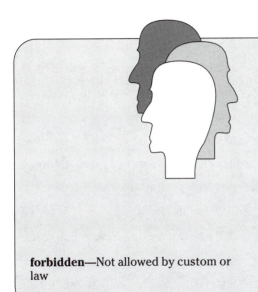

# CULTURE CAPSULE

From our parents and our culture we learn what is considered good to eat and what is considered bad, what is permitted and what is forbidden. In the United States, no one eats dogs and most people will not eat horse meat. Some foods, although not taboo, are not common either. So some Americans will not eat snails or raw fish, for example.

Certain religious groups have taboos—pork for Jews and Moslems, beef for Hindus. Even individuals may decide not to eat certain foods. People who object to animals being killed may be vegetarians and refuse to eat meat.

**forbidden**—Not allowed by custom or law

# Cultural Exchange

*A. Tell whether these sentences about the United States are true or false.*

1. Americans enjoy eating dogs.

2. They do not like to eat horse meat.

3. Some people may refuse to eat any meat at all.

4. Snails and raw fish are popular foods.

5. Different religious groups follow their own food taboos.

*B. Answer these questions about your culture in writing or aloud.*

1. What food taboos are there, if any?

2. What foods are not taboo but people do not eat them very often? Why?

3. What are some favorite main dishes?

4. What are some favorite desserts?

5. What are some favorite snacks?

6. What are some typical breakfast foods?

7. What are some favorite holiday foods?

***C.*** *Discuss these questions with your classmates.*

1. What food(s) would you never eat because of religious or family beliefs?

2. When you were a child what food did you refuse to eat that you now like?

3. What new food have you most recently learned to eat?

4. What is your favorite food from your own culture?

5. What American foods would you like to try that you have not eaten before?

6. What American foods do you already enjoy?

7. What American foods have you tried and didn't like?

8. What American foods would you never taste because you are sure you would not like them?

# Expansion

*Make a survey of foods that people do not like to eat. Talk to five people outside the classroom. Ask them questions about each of the foods below.*

1. Have you ever eaten . . . ?

2. If so, did you like it/them? *or* If not, would you be willing to eat it/them?

   There are four different ways to answer the questions:

   a. Yes, I like to eat it/them.

   b. Yes, but I didn't like it/them.

   c. No, but I'd be willing to eat it/them.

   d. No, and I wouldn't be willing to eat it/them.

   **Foods**

   | | | |
   |---|---|---|
   | dog meat | frog's legs | snake |
   | horse meat | bear's paw | pork |
   | snails | calf's liver | corn on the cob |
   | raw fish | animal intestine | peanut butter |
   | alligator | oysters | raw vegetable salad |
   | hot dogs | beef | cheese |
   | milk | brains | monkey meat |
   | pizza | ants | yogurt |
   | sheep's eye | beef tongue | noodles with tomato sauce |

3. After you finish your survey, compare your answers with your classmates' answers. Are their answers similar or very different?

# Follow-Up

**A.** *Give a brief oral or written report. Choose number 1 or 2.*

1. Tell about the time when you were introduced to the most unusual food you ever ate.

2. Tell about a time when you introduced or tried to introduce someone to a food that person had never eaten.

*When you describe the event, consider including some of the following details:*

How long ago did this happen? How old were you?

Where were you living at the time?

Describe the occasion. (a meal at home? a meal in a restaurant? a simple meal? a family banquet?)

Describe the food. How was it prepared?

What did the food look like? How did it taste?

*If you choose number 1, also consider including some of the following details:*

Did someone have to convince you to eat the food? Did you enjoy it or not?

Have you ever eaten it again? Would you ever eat it again? If not, why not?

*If you choose number 2, also consider including some of the following details:*

Why hadn't the other person ever eaten this food?

Did the other person try the food? If so, did he or she enjoy it?

If the other person would not eat the food, how did you feel about that?

Did this experience affect your relationship with the other person in any way? If so, how?

**B.** *Create a one-page advertisement for your favorite food. Use colorful words to describe how it tastes, looks, and makes you feel when you eat it. You can also include a drawing to show how good it looks.*

*Pin or tape your advertisement to the wall with your classmates' advertisements. How many of you chose the same foods?*

# UNIT 5

# *Eating Out*

## ? Do you know...

1.  In the United States which foods can be eaten without using any utensils?

2.  Have you ever been confused about which utensil to use or how to use it?

# Eating the Western Way

*Read the story.*

I was born in Vietnam and since both of my parents are Chinese, most of the things I do are based on Chinese customs. However, I have lived in the United States for a long time so I have also picked up many American ways, but I still use my Chinese name, Yen.

The one thing I find very difficult to get used to is the eating utensils. In many American restaurants there are two forks, two spoons, and two knives. I get really confused trying to find out which utensil I should use for which kind of food. And not long ago, I didn't know how to use a knife and fork at all.

In my culture the two items we use for eating are a pair of chopsticks and a soup spoon. Chopsticks are long skinny sticks made out of wood called bamboo. We use them to pick up our food. The soup spoon is oval in shape and is usually made out of porcelain. We use it to sip our soup or to scoop our food.

Two years ago, my boyfriend invited me to the Christmas party given by his company. He told me that it was going to be a dinner party at the Sheraton Hotel and that I should dress formally. The week before the party, I went shopping for a pretty dress to wear. I had a hard time because I didn't really know how Americans would dress for this occasion. Well, luckily for me, a salesgirl gave me her opinion and I found just the right dress. Then came the day of the party. Knowing I was properly dressed, I felt very comfortable. My boyfriend introduced me to his co-workers, and we were seated at a table with four other American couples. Then I looked down at my knife and fork, and my heart sank. I had wanted to ask my boyfriend how to use the utensils for what I called "Eating the Western Way." But I had been so worried about what to wear that I had forgotten. Now, seated at the table with the other couples, I would have to figure out the utensils for

**utensils**—Objects that are used to cut and eat food

**porcelain**—A thin, shiny material of very fine quality that is produced by baking a clay mixture myself. Everything went fine until the lady who was sitting next to me noticed that I kept watching what everyone was doing and switching my fork and knife from one hand to another. She started to laugh and said, "Oh dear, don't be so nervous. Let me show you how to use your knife."

At this point my face was red and I didn't know what to say. Usually Chinese people aren't allowed to have a knife on the table. I was still a little scared to hold the knife and now I was also nervous and embarrassed about the whole situation. I ended up letting my boyfriend cut the steak for me. As for the lady who was sitting next to me, I was too embarrassed to look at her or thank her for offering to help.

Since then, my boyfriend has taken me to many American restaurants. Not only have I gotten used to eating the food, but he has taught me how to eat the Western way. Now I have no problem handling my knife and fork, but it makes me smile sometimes when I think of how embarrassing it once was.

# Comprehension

**A.** *Tell whether these sentences are true or false.*

1. Yen has had trouble getting used to American utensils.
2. In Yen's culture two kinds of utensils are used for eating.
3. Yen had no trouble shopping for a formal dress.
4. The salesgirl was rude to Yen.
5. The lady next to Yen at the dinner tried to help her.
6. Yen let the lady help her.
7. Yen's boyfriend cut her steak.
8. Now Yen has no problem handling her knife and fork.

**B.** *Answer these questions.*

1. What does Yen find confusing about the utensils in American restaurants?
2. What utensils are used in Yen's culture?
3. Where was the dinner party held?
4. How did Yen feel about the dress she wore?
5. What is "Eating the Western Way"?
6. How did Yen learn to become good at eating the Western way?

### C. *Give your opinion.*

1. When the lady at the table laughed at Yen, do you think she was making fun of her?

2. Do you think it was kind of the lady to help, or do you think she was interfering?

3. Do you think Yen's boyfriend was right to cut her steak for her? Why or why not?

4. If you were in Yen's place, what would you have done that night?

### D. *Now add your own ideas to the story.*

1. Is Yen embarrassed or grateful when the lady offers to cut her meat?

2. Is Yen embarrassed or relieved when her boyfriend cuts the meat?

3. Is the boyfriend grateful to the lady for offering to help Yen, or is he resentful?

4. Is the lady angry or disappointed when Yen does not look at her or will not let her help? Does she understand how Yen feels?

5. Do Yen and her boyfriend ever talk to the lady? If they do, what do they say?

### E. *Compare yourself with Yen.*

1. What did Yen learn?

2. What did you learn from Yen's story?

# Vocabulary

*What is the meaning of the underlined word or phrase? Circle the letter of the correct answer.*

1. I get really confused about American utensils.
   a. I understand how to use American utensils.
   b. I have difficulty in understanding how to use American utensils.

2. My boyfriend cut the steak for me.
   a. My boyfriend used a knife to slice the meat into smaller pieces.
   b. My boyfriend moved the meat from my plate to his.

3. Chopsticks are long skinny sticks.
   a. Chopsticks are long wooden sticks.
   b. Chopsticks are long thin sticks.

4. A salesgirl gave me her opinion.
   a. A salesgirl told me to make up my own mind.
   b. A salesgirl gave me advice.

*Continued on the following page*

5. Americans <u>switch</u> forks and knives from one hand to another.
   a. Americans change the forks and knives from one hand to another.
   b. Americans decide ahead of time which hand will hold the fork and which hand will hold the knife.

6. Yen had difficulty in using <u>American eating utensils.</u>
   a. Yen had difficulty in eating American foods.
   b. Yen had difficulty in using a fork and knife.

7. Most of what Yen does is <u>based on Chinese customs.</u>
   a. Yen mostly wears Chinese costumes.
   b. Yen mostly follows Chinese traditions.

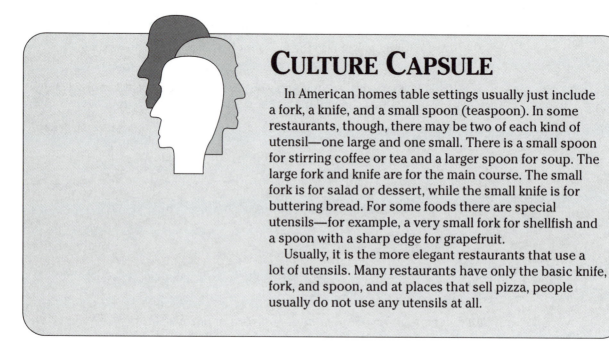

# CULTURE CAPSULE

In American homes table settings usually just include a fork, a knife, and a small spoon (teaspoon). In some restaurants, though, there may be two of each kind of utensil—one large and one small. There is a small spoon for stirring coffee or tea and a larger spoon for soup. The large fork and knife are for the main course. The small fork is for salad or dessert, while the small knife is for buttering bread. For some foods there are special utensils—for example, a very small fork for shellfish and a spoon with a sharp edge for grapefruit.

Usually, it is the more elegant restaurants that use a lot of utensils. Many restaurants have only the basic knife, fork, and spoon, and at places that sell pizza, people usually do not use any utensils at all.

# Cultural ⫸ ⫷ Exchange

***A.*** *Tell whether these sentences about the United States are true or false.*

1. The small spoon is used for drinking soup.

2. The large spoon is for stirring tea or coffee.

3. Americans usually eat pizza with their hands.

4. Small forks are for salad or dessert.

5. Small knives are used for eating shellfish.

*B.* Fill in the chart below, and then share your answers with your classmates.

| In a Restaurant in Your Country . . . | |
|---|---|
| What foods can be eaten with fingers? | |
| How do people get the food server's attention? | |
| How do people express appreciation for the meal? (sounds? words?) | |
| What words do people say to make a toast (pay tribute to the host, the food, or the occasion)? | |
| Do people leave the food server a tip? How much? | |

**make a toast**—To drink and wish out loud for success and happiness

**tip**—Money left for food servers by satisfied customers; usually 15–20% of the check

*C.* Discuss these questions with your classmates.

1. What does a typical table setting look like in your culture? On a piece of paper, draw plates, bowls, drinking glasses or cups, and utensils in their usual positions. Explain the table setting.

2. From what you have learned, what does a typical table setting look like in American culture? On a piece of paper, draw plates, bowls, drinking glasses or cups, and utensils in their usual positions. Explain the table setting.

3. In your culture what foods are you allowed to eat while standing or walking? From what you have learned or seen in movies or on TV, in the United States what foods can you eat while standing or walking?

4. In your family are children taken out to eat with adults? If so, how are they expected to behave? From what you know, have read about, or have seen in movies or on TV, do many Americans take their children out to eat? How do their children behave?

5. How often do you eat out? In what kinds of places do you eat? Do you enjoy eating out, or do you prefer to eat at home?

# Expansion

*Draw a line from the food in the left-hand column to the appropriate description in the right-hand column.*

Brownie

Caesar salad

Club sandwich

Fish sticks

French toast

Hot dog

Pancakes

Sloppy joe

Submarine (hero) sandwich

Waldorf salad

Pot roast

Ground beef with chili sauce poured over a roll

Bread dipped in egg batter and then fried

A large cut of beef cooked for a long time with vegetables in a liquid

Lettuce with anchovies, with a dressing of lemon juice, seasonings, olive oil, and raw egg, and with bread croutons and Parmesan cheese on top

Fish filets cut in finger shapes, breaded, and fried

A rich chocolate cake square, often with nuts inside

Meat sausage in a bun, often eaten with mustard and relish

Cold meats and cheese, often with lettuce, tomatoes, peppers, and seasonings, served on a long roll

A three-layered toasted sandwich, often filled with chicken or turkey, lettuce, tomatoes, and bacon

Flat fried cakes, often eaten with syrup

Cut-up apples, celery, and nuts mixed in a mayonnaise dressing

# Follow-Up ✓

**A.** *Give a brief oral or written report. Choose number 1 or 2.*

1. Tell about a time when you were eating in a restaurant and something was wrong with the food and you did something about it.

2. Tell about a time in a restaurant when you found something wrong with the check and you did something about it.

*When you describe the event, consider including some of the following details:*

When did this happen?

Where were you living at the time?

What was the restaurant called?

What was wrong with the food or the check?

What did you do about it?

What did the restaurant do about it?

Were you satisfied with the results?

Have you ever returned to that restaurant?

**B.** *Ordering at the restaurant: Collect some menus from local restaurants. Work in groups of three to five. One person is the food server who takes the order and makes out the check. The rest of the group are the customers who order the food, check the bill, and figure out the 15 percent tip. You can ask for individual checks or you may want to practice "splitting the check." Here are typical food-server questions and responses:*

"Are you ready to order?"

"What would you like this evening?"

"Hi. My name is _____. May I bring you something to drink before you order?"

"Will there be anything else?"

"Thank you and come again."

*Here are typical questions and responses from customers:*

"What's today's special?"

"Is there anything you would recommend?"

"We're ready to order now."

"May we have our check?"

**special**—In a restaurant, food not regularly offered or food that has a lower price than usual

# UNIT 6

# *Guests and Hosts*

## ? Do you know...

**1.** What do you usually bring to someone's home if you are invited for dinner?

**2.** What is a potluck meal?

# Potluck

*Read the story.*

My name is Tai and I was born in the southern part of China. After receiving a B.A. degree, I taught English in Beijing and later became an interpreter. Now I am in the United States to get a degree in marketing.

When I first came to this country, everything seemed strange and different. For example, people often said hello to each other even if they were strangers. In China, only friends say hello when they meet. But of all the cultural differences, one in particular came as a surprise to me. An American friend invited me to a dinner party at her home. A day before the party, I happened to talk to a Chinese friend. He asked me what food I was bringing to the party. I had no idea what he was talking about. In China, the hosts prepare all the food and drinks—the only thing that the guests bring is their mouths to eat with. My friend explained to me that the dinner party was a potluck. He said that at a potluck dinner party each guest brings food and everybody shares the food. It was lucky that I talked to this friend before the dinner. I had just planned to bring a bottle of liquor, and I would have felt embarrassed. Instead, I made some typical Chinese food for the potluck, and everyone there really liked it.

As I've learned, many dinners in the United States aren't potlucks. They are more like our Chinese dinners. Guests may bring a bottle of wine or a small gift, but the hosts provide the meal. However, I've also come to like the custom of potlucks. Since everyone helps out, potlucks make it easy to have dinner with friends more often. This is especially useful since so many women today work and have less time to cook large meals. By now I've explained this custom to many Chinese friends here. And when I'm invited to a potluck, I always do my best to bring some typical Chinese food.

**B.A. degree**—Bachelor of Arts certificate, usually received after completing four years of college courses

**interpreter**—A person who puts the words of one language into the words of another language, usually by talking

**marketing**—How goods are advertised and sold

**typical**—Characteristic or common

# Comprehension

**A.** *Tell whether these sentences are true or false.*

1. In China, only friends say hello to each other when they meet.
2. Tai was planning to give a dinner party.
3. He did not know what *potluck* meant.
4. Potluck is the name of a delicious Chinese food.
5. In China, hosts provide all the food and drink.
6. In the United States, hosts often provide all the food and drink.
7. Tai does not like potlucks.
8. Americans do not like potluck dinner parties because they are too much work.

**B.** *Answer these questions.*

1. What does potluck mean?
2. Who explained potluck to Tai?
3. Originally, what did Tai plan to bring to the party?
4. What is the Chinese custom for dinner parties?
5. What kind of food does Tai like to bring to potlucks?
6. Who has Tai explained the potluck custom to?

**C.** *Give your opinion.*

1. Tai says that for him potlucks were one of the most surprising American customs. Do you find the custom of potluck surprising? What American customs have surprised you the most?
2. Tai says he would have been very embarrassed if he had gone to the potluck without food. Do you agree that this would have been embarrassing? Explain your answer.
3. Have you ever been to a potluck? Which do you prefer—potlucks or regular dinner parties where the hosts do all the work?
4. How do you think Tai's Chinese friends react when he explains potluck to them? Why do you think so?
5. Do you think Tai has a positive or a negative attitude about living in a new culture? Explain.

***D.*** *Now add your own ideas to the story.*

1. Why did Tai's friend tell him about the potluck custom?

2. How did Tai feel when he learned about potluck?

3. When Tai brought Chinese food for the potluck, what did his American hostess think?

4. How did Tai feel when he brought the Chinese food?

***E.*** *Compare yourself with Tai.*

1. What did Tai learn?

2. What did you learn from Tai's story?

# Vocabulary ▌▌▌➤

*What is the meaning of the underlined word or phrase? Circle the letter of the correct answer.*

1. Tai's friend explained that the dinner party was a <u>potluck</u>.
   a. At the dinner party they would be using a special lucky pot.
   b. At the dinner party the guests would bring food to share.

2. Hosts <u>provide the meal</u>.
   a. The persons who invite the guests supply the food.
   b. Each guest brings food.

3. Tai likes to bring <u>typical</u> Chinese food.
   a. Tai likes to bring food that most Chinese people eat.
   b. Tai likes to bring unusual Chinese food.

4. In Beijing Tai became an <u>interpreter</u>.
   a. Tai translated languages.
   b. Tai became a dancer.

5. Tai had planned to bring <u>liquor</u>.
   a. Tai had planned to bring some licorice candy.
   b. Tai had planned to bring an alcoholic beverage.

6. Everything seemed <u>strange</u>.
   a. Everything seemed unfamiliar.
   b. Everything seemed tense, strained.

# CULTURE CAPSULE

Although friends and neighbors sometimes "drop in," usually Americans do not visit one another without an invitation. If you are invited to someone's home for dinner, the invitation might be only for you and your spouse. Do not bring your children or parents unless they were invited or you have asked the host. Do not arrive earlier than the time mentioned and try not to be too late.

You might ask your hosts if you can bring something. If they say no, then you can still bring a small gift—for example, flowers, a box of candy, or a bottle of wine. If you are invited to a potluck, of course, you are expected to bring some food.

**spouse**—A person's husband or wife

# Cultural ▶ ◀ Exchange

**A.** *Tell whether these sentences about the United States are true or false.*

1. Friends and neighbors never drop in.

2. It is impolite to bring a gift to your host.

3. It is better not to bring your children unless the hosts have asked you to.

4. Your hosts won't mind if you bring your parents.

5. If you are invited for dinner at 6:00 P.M., you should arrive at 5:30.

**B.** *Answer these questions in writing or aloud about being invited to dinner in your culture.*

1. What do people usually bring to the hosts?

2. When is the best time to arrive? Is it best to be early (how many minutes)? To be late (how many minutes)? Or to arrive at exactly the time the host has requested?

3. How soon do people begin eating? Right away? Or do they wait, and for how long?

4. What do guests do or say if the food is delicious? When do they say it?

5. If a guest is still hungry and would like more food, how many times must the host offer the food before the guest may accept it?

6. Is there something guests do with their utensils or food to indicate that they want no more to eat? Is there something guests say to indicate they want no more food?

7. Is it acceptable or impolite to refuse to eat some of the food?

8. When finished eating, should guests leave some food on the plate or leave the plate empty?

9. What is one thing people should never do at the table?

10. When do people leave the premises? Right after eating? About an hour after eating? Other?

11. What do people say when leaving?

**C.** *Discuss these questions with your classmates.*

1. In your culture do guests offer to help serve the food or clear the table? Do you think this is the same or different in the United States?

2. In your culture what are some favorite topics of conversation at dinner parties?

3. Do men and women eat separately? If they eat together, do the women and men usually separate after dinner?

4. If small children are invited to a dinner party, where do they sit: Separately? Next to the mother? Next to the father? Between the two? Who takes care of them during the meal: Father? Mother? Both?

5. In your culture who usually cooks the food for a dinner party?

6. In your culture is alcohol served at dinner parties? If so, what kind? Is it served before eating? During the meal? After the meal? If no alcohol is served, what other kinds of beverages do people drink?

7. Do you think that dinner parties in the United States are basically similar to dinner parties in your country, or are they quite different? To your knowledge, what are the biggest differences?

# Expansion

*Draw a line from the word or words in the left-hand column to the appropriate definition in the right-hand column.*

Barbecue

Black-tie event

Brunch

Grace

Hors d'oeuvres (appetizers)

BYOB

Potluck

Regrets only

RSVP

Toasts

Small amounts of food that generally accompany drinks before dinner; for example, tiny sandwiches, chips, and dips

Drinking in honor of the host or a guest; glasses are raised as words of praise are said

Generally held outdoors, in a backyard or in a park; food is cooked over hot coals

A party to which men and women must wear formal clothes; for example, a man would wear a dinner jacket and tie or a tuxedo

Each guest brings some food to the meal

You must let the host know whether or not you plan to attend

You only have to let your host know if you are not coming to the party

Bring your own bottle of wine or something to drink

A combination meal of breakfast and lunch usually served between 11:00 A.M. and 1:00 P.M.

A short prayer spoken aloud or silently just before food is eaten

# Follow-Up ✔

A. *Give a brief oral or written report. Choose number 1 or 2.*

1. Tell about a time when you hosted a meal and one of your guests did something surprising.

2. Tell about a time when you were a guest at a party and either you or one of the other guests did something that was embarrassing.

*In your report, consider including some of the following details:*

> When did this happen?
>
> Where were you living at the time?
>
> What was your role (guest or host)?
>
> What was the occasion?
>
> What went wrong?
>
> How did you react?
>
> How did others react?
>
> Did anyone learn anything from this experience? Explain.

**B.** *Write a thank-you note to someone who invited you to a dinner party. It was an elegant dinner party, and you really enjoyed it because your host paid special attention to you and made you feel welcome.*

# UNIT 7

# *Confusing Phrases*

## ? Do you know...

**1.** What does it mean when someone is "pulling your leg" or when someone asks you to "shake a leg" or tells you to "break a leg"?

**2.** What other American phrases have confused you?

# Quit Pulling My Leg

*Read the story.*

My name is Lorenzo and I was born in Mexico City, but I've been living here in the United States for five years. While in the tenth grade I had an incident with my ESL teacher, Mrs. Del Signore.

It all began one night when I stayed up until midnight doing homework for the next day. When I finished, I put the homework paper on the dinner table and went to sleep. The next morning I woke up late and was in such a hurry to get to school on time that I forgot to take my homework.

In my ESL class, Mrs. Del Signore said, "Pass your homework to the front of your row." Today, like every day, she used the homework to take attendance. So, after a few minutes, she asked, "Lorenzo Gonzales is not here?" I answered, "I'm here."

She turned and looked at me and called me to her desk to ask me about the homework. When I explained what had happened, she answered, "Quit pulling my leg. I want the truth."

I felt my face turning red. What she said didn't make any sense. I wasn't close enough to pull her leg. Besides, she was sitting at her desk, and it would have been practically impossible to pull her leg from under the desk. The whole class looked at her because they did not understand her either. I'm sure I had a perplexed look on my face. When Mrs. Del Signore noticed it, she immediately realized the reason and apologized to me and the rest of the class. She explained what she meant by "pulling my leg." She had thought I was kidding her about the homework, that I was just making up a story.

The next day she discussed idioms. We were eager to learn them, since we could clearly see they would come in handy sooner or later. As a result of this experience, to this day whenever I hear an idiom I do not understand, I simply go to my old high school and ask my friend Mrs. Del Signore.

**perplexed**—Confused

**come in handy**—To be useful or convenient

# Comprehension

**A.** *Tell whether these sentences are true or false.*

1. Lorenzo forgot to do his ESL homework.

2. Lorenzo overslept the next morning.

3. Mrs. Del Signore uses the homework to take attendance.

4. Lorenzo could not really pull Mrs. Del Signore's leg, because she was sitting at her desk.

5. Lorenzo was the only student who did not understand what his teacher meant.

6. "Pulling a leg" is an idiom that means to arrive late.

7. Lorenzo likes Mrs. Del Signore.

**B.** *Answer these questions.*

1. Why did Lorenzo forget his homework?

2. What was Lorenzo's reaction when his teacher said, "Quit pulling my leg"?

3. What does "Quit pulling my leg" mean?

4. What did Mrs. Del Signore do to help her students?

5. What does Lorenzo do now when he does not understand an idiom?

**C.** *Give your opinion.*

1. Do you think Lorenzo is a good student? Why?

2. Do you think Mrs. Del Signore is a good teacher? Why?

3. What do you think Mrs. Del Signore learned from this experience?

4. Suppose your teacher used an idiom you did not understand. What would you do? What would you do if a friend used an idiom you did not understand?

**D.** *Now add your own ideas to the story.*

1. Is Mrs. Del Signore angry or sympathetic about Lorenzo not having his homework?

2. When Mrs. Del Signore calls Lorenzo to her desk, does he feel guilty, frightened, or embarrassed about leaving his work home?

3. Does Mrs. Del Signore believe Lorenzo did his homework?

**E.** *Compare yourself with Lorenzo.*

1. What did Lorenzo learn?

2. What did you learn from Lorenzo's story?

# Vocabulary

*What is the meaning of the underlined word? Circle the letter of the correct answer.*

1. Lorenzo <u>forgot</u> to take his homework to school.
   a. He brought his homework to school.
   b. He left his homework in his house.

2. Mrs. Del Signore asked Lorenzo about his <u>homework</u>.
   a. She asked him about the work he does at home such as making his bed and helping his mother in the kitchen.
   b. She asked him about the schoolwork he was supposed to do at home.

3. Mrs. Del Signore thought Lorenzo was <u>kidding</u> her.
   a. She thought he was fooling her.
   b. She thought he was being childish.

4. The next day Mrs. Del Signore discussed <u>idioms</u>.
   a. She talked about people who have a very low intelligence.
   b. She talked about phrases that have an unexpected meaning.

5. Mrs. Del Signore <u>apologized</u> to Lorenzo.
   a. Mrs. Del Signore said she was sorry.
   b. Mrs. Del Signore said she was angry.

6. The teacher used the homework to take <u>attendance</u>.
   a. She used the homework to find out which students were absent.
   b. She used the homework to mark their grades in her book.

7. Lorenzo was in a <u>hurry</u> to get to school.
   a. He rushed.
   b. He relaxed.

## CULTURE CAPSULE

There are many idioms about legs in American English. "Pulling someone's leg" means not telling that person the truth. To "shake a leg" means to hurry, and if someone tells you to "break a leg," it means he or she is wishing you good luck.

Other parts of the body are also frequently used in idioms. "Don't lose your head" means to stay calm. To have "sticky fingers" means to steal. To "win by a hair" means to barely win, and if someone says you're "wet behind the ears," it means you lack experience.

# Cultural ⟶ Exchange

**A.** *Tell whether these sentences about the United States are true or false.*

1. "Shake a leg" means to hurry.

2. "Sticky fingers" means the person has just eaten candy.

3. You're "wet behind the ears" means you didn't dry yourself carefully after your bath.

4. "Break a leg" is a good-luck wish.

5. "Don't lose your head" means don't get excited.

**B.** *Here is a list of idioms and their meanings. What do you have in your language that is comparable?*

| Idiom | Meaning | Your language |
|---|---|---|
| A long face | To be sad | |
| Let your hair down | Relax | |
| Pain in the neck | Someone or something that causes a problem | |
| Face the music | Confront an issue | |
| Get off someone's back | Stop bothering a person | |
| Keep an eye on | Watch | |
| Heart of gold | To be generous | |

**C.** *Discuss these questions with your classmates.*

1. What American idioms seem especially interesting to you?

2. Which American idioms are difficult for you to understand?

3. Which idioms do you like to use from your own language?

4. Have you ever used an idiom in your own language that your parents or children did not understand? Describe.

5. Do you know of any American idioms that correspond to the ones you use in your own language?

# Expansion

*Choose one of the following American idioms or proverbs, or think of one of your own. If you do not understand the meaning, look it up in a dictionary. Draw a picture of what the idiom or proverb describes. Then show the drawing to your classmates to determine whether they know which idiom or proverb you have drawn and what it really means.*

He's a chip off the old block.

The cold shoulder

It's raining cats and dogs.

Out of the frying pan, into the fire

Kill two birds with one stone

Getting ripped off

Don't bite the hand that feeds you.

Hit the nail on the head

Money is burning a hole in your pocket.

He's a wolf in sheep's clothing.

Bury the hatchet

# Follow-Up

**A.** *Give a brief oral or written report. Choose number 1 or 2.*

1. Tell about a time when you misunderstood the meaning of words in your own language or another language.

2. Tell about a time when something you said was misunderstood by someone else.

*In your report, consider including some of the following details:*

When did this happen? How old were you?

Where were you living at the time?

Who was the person who was confused?

In what language was the misunderstood phrase? Was it a difference in language?

What was the misunderstood phrase?

What was the real meaning of the words?

What did you or the other person think the words meant?

How did the person who misunderstood react?

What happened as a result of the misunderstanding?

How did the misunderstanding get cleared up?

**B.** *Work with two other students and make a list of American phrases that have caused you some confusion. Compare your list with those of your classmates.*

# UNIT 8
# *Greetings*

## ? Do you know...

1. How do friends in the United States greet each other?

2. How do Americans greet one another in business settings?

# Hand Kissing

*Read the story.*

My name is Cristina. I was born in Mexico and came to the United States when I was three months old. Even though we lived in the United States, my parents raised my brother, my sisters, and me just as they had been raised in Mexico—with very strict rules. My parents taught us we should respect grandparents more than anyone in the world because grandparents had lived the longest. They had more knowledge about life, and no matter what they said, even if it didn't make sense, they were right. We were taught that to hug or kiss grandparents was disrespectful and that we should greet them by kissing their hand. When you are young, you think that everyone lives and thinks just like you do. Well, I soon found out this isn't true.

My best friend in third grade was the first close friend I had who was raised in the American way. This friend invited me to her birthday party. I was very excited because I had never been invited to a friend's birthday party before.

The day of the party came, and I was happy but at the same time very nervous. I thought of all the people who would be there. I wanted her family to like me. Slowly, I walked up to the house. Finally, I got to the door and rang the bell. My friend came running out with a big smile, telling me she was happy that I came. She let me in and introduced me to her parents. They smiled and said hello. Then she said, "Come here. I want you to meet my grandpa."

I followed her into the living room where her grandfather was sitting. She introduced us and he reached out his hand. He was going to shake hands, but I thought he was expecting me to kiss his hand, so I did.

I noticed that he looked at me in a strange way, as if he didn't like what I had done. Everyone else in the room looked at me, and my friend started laughing. I was very confused. I didn't know what I had done wrong. I sat down and tried to figure out what

**strict**—Severe; requiring complete obedience

happened. Just then, a little boy ran to my friend's grandfather and jumped on his lap. The little boy started to hug and kiss the grandfather. When I saw this, I got up and took the little boy by the hand and said, "No." I guess I said it pretty loudly because the room became very silent and all eyes were on me.

The next day at school my friend asked me why I acted so strangely at her party. She asked me why I kissed her grandfather's hand and why I told the little boy to get away from his grandfather. I explained my customs to her and she explained hers to me. Fortunately, we stayed very good friends.

# Comprehension

*A. Tell whether these sentences are true or false.*

1. Cristina had very many American friends.

2. Cristina's parents let their children follow whatever customs they desired.

3. In Cristina's culture grandparents were highly respected because they had lived the longest and knew the most.

4. Cristina loved to hug and kiss her grandparents.

5. At the party the grandfather was surprised when Cristina kissed his hand.

6. The little boy kissed the grandfather's hand too.

7. The party guests were very surprised by Cristina's behavior.

8. After this incident, Cristina's friendship with her classmate ended.

*B. Answer these questions.*

1. Why couldn't Cristina hug or kiss her grandparents?

2. What was the correct form when greeting them?

3. What kind of greeting was her friend's grandfather used to getting from his grandchildren?

4. What kind of greeting did he expect from Cristina?

5. Why did Cristina say "No" to the little boy?

6. Why did the room become silent?

***C.*** *Give your opinion.*

1. Why do you think Cristina's parents continued to follow their Mexican traditions even though they lived in the United States?

2. Do you think Cristina's parents made a good decision about keeping their Mexican traditions? Why or why not?

3. To help ease the situation, what might the grandfather have said to Cristina after she kissed his hand?

4. What do you think the party guests thought about Cristina?

5. Do you think it was a good idea for Cristina's girlfriend to ask her why she acted so strangely at the party? Why or why not?

***D.*** *Now add your own ideas to the story.*

1. How did the little boy feel when Cristina said "No" to him?

2. What did the grandfather think about Cristina when she kissed his hand?

3. Did Cristina stay long at the party, or did she leave early?

4. If Cristina stayed at the party, how did the other guests treat her?

5. Is Cristina's friend sorry she invited her?

6. Will Cristina's friend get into trouble for inviting her to the party?

***E.*** *Compare yourself with Cristina.*

1. What did Cristina learn?

2. What did you learn from Cristina's story?

# Vocabulary ||||▶

*What is the meaning of the underlined word? Circle the letter of the correct answer.*

1. The room became <u>silent</u>.
   a. The room became cold.
   b. The room became quiet.

2. Cristina was <u>introduced</u> to her friend's parents.
   a. Cristina was presented to her friend's parents.
   b. The parents of Cristina's friend gave Cristina a gift.

3. Cristina was <u>invited</u> to a birthday party.
   a. Cristina hosted a birthday party.
   b. Cristina was asked to attend a birthday party.

4. Cristina was taught that it was <u>disrespectful</u> to hug and kiss grandparents.
   a. Cristina was supposed to hug and kiss her grandparents.
   b. Cristina was not supposed to hug and kiss her grandparents.

5. Cristina's grandparents had more <u>knowledge</u> about life.
   a. The grandparents were older.
   b. The grandparents knew more.

6. Cristina thought the grandfather was <u>expecting</u> her to kiss his hand.
   a. She thought he wanted her to kiss his hand.
   b. She thought he didn't want her to kiss his hand.

7. Cristina was <u>excited</u> about going to the birthday party.
   a. She couldn't make up her mind about whether or not she should go to the party.
   b. She was happy about going to the party.

# CULTURE CAPSULE

In the United States the form of greeting depends on how well people know each other and on the situation. When people are first introduced, they usually shake hands. Handshakes are especially common in business or formal situations.

When two women friends meet, they might hug and kiss one another on the cheek. (Although in many cultures people kiss on both cheeks, Americans usually just kiss on one cheek.) Male friends would not kiss but might embrace for a moment. A male friend and female friend might kiss on the cheek, even though they are not romantically involved. If people know each other but not well, they might just say hello. Friends often do this, too. A stranger might greet an older person with a handshake. A grandchild would probably greet his or her grandparents with hugs and kisses.

**embrace**—To hold closely and affectionately in one's arms; to hug

**romantically involved**—In a love relationship; boyfriend and girlfriend

# Cultural Exchange

**A.** *Tell whether these sentences about the United States are true or false.*

1. Handshakes are common in both social and business situations.

2. Two women greet each other only with handshakes.

3. Americans usually kiss on both cheeks.

4. A man and woman might kiss each other on the cheek, even if they are not related.

5. Generally, grandchildren don't kiss their grandparents' hands.

**B.** For each of the situations listed below, which form of greeting does your culture use: Pat on the arm? Slap on the back? Bow? Hug? Kiss? Nod? Handshake? Other?

| In Your Country How Do People Greet . . . | |
|---|---|
| Parents? | |
| Brothers and sisters? | |
| Grandparents? | |
| A boss? | |
| A spouse? In public? In private? | |
| A sweetheart? In public? In private? | |
| A friend of the same sex? | |
| A friend of the opposite sex? | |

**C.** Discuss these questions with your classmates.

1. How do you greet a stranger?

2. In your culture, what are the rules for handshaking? Do you use a loose or a firm grip? Do women shake hands with women? Do women shake hands with men? If you are in a large group and must shake hands, who is the first person whose hand you must shake? Who comes next?

3. In your culture, what is the meaning of a smile? Do you smile at strangers? At friends? How is this the same as or different from American smiling habits?

4. What do you think you would find difficult to get used to about American greeting customs?

5. Do you prefer the greeting customs in your culture or in American culture? Or do you prefer some from each culture? Explain your answer.

# Expansion

*With one or two partners, practice some American greetings for the following situations. Then perform the greetings for your classmates. Some examples of words you might use to go along with the greetings are given below. You can also make up your own.*

1. Good friends who have not seen each other in a few weeks

2. Co-workers who unexpectedly see each other at the shopping mall

3. An aunt greeting her niece

4. A boss introducing a new employee to other employees

"Hello, how are you?"

"I'm fine, thank you."

"You look wonderful."

"I'm pleased to meet you."

"I've really missed you."

# Follow-Up ✓

*A. Give a brief oral or written report. Choose number 1 or 2.*

1. Tell about a time when you were greeted in a very unexpected way or were expected to greet someone in a way that was difficult for you.

2. Tell about a time when you observed a greeting custom that was different.

*In your report, consider including some of the following details:*

When did it happen?

How old were you?

Where were you living at the time?

What were the cultural backgrounds of the people involved?

What greeting behavior was expected?

Describe the greeting. What was different about it?

How did those individuals involved react to the situation?

*B. Write a letter to a friend from your culture who is planning to visit the United States. Give some good advice about the accepted greeting customs. Are there any greeting customs from your culture that might be misunderstood in the United States? Tell your friend to avoid these greeting customs.*

# UNIT 9

# *Forms of Address*

## ? Do you know...

**1.** What kinds of people would you address by their first name? What kinds of people would you address by a title (Mr., Ms., etc.) and last name?

**2.** How are teachers addressed in the United States?

# What Should I Call You?

*Read the story.*

My name is Yuan. As a student in Taiwan for the first ten years of my school life, I learned to respect teachers. I was taught that it is not respectful to call teachers by their name, that they should always be addressed by the title "Teacher."

Seven years ago, when I moved to the United States, I entered an ESL class in a local high school. The students kept calling the teacher "Miss White." I felt that they were being disrespectful, but because of my problems with English, I couldn't ask them about it.

Time passed. I found that often when I asked questions, Miss White seemed annoyed and said something, but I was not able to understand what she said. I wondered if I had done something that was not respectful or if somehow I hadn't been a good student. Finally, one day when I raised my hand and said, "Excuse me, Teacher . . . ," Miss White interrupted me before I could finish my question. With a not-so-happy face, she said, "Teacher is my title at work. Teacher is not my name. My name is Miss White."

Now I was completely confused. Why would she want me to call her by her name? Why would she get so upset when I was trying to be respectful? I wanted to ask her the reason but my English was still not good enough.

I was angry and sad for a few days, until my uncle returned from Taiwan. I asked him, "Why do people get upset simply because I am trying to respect them?" He asked me to tell him the whole story. I told him what happened in school. He told me that what was right back in Taiwan was not necessarily proper here in the United States. He also told me that I should not be sad and that I should try to understand what is done here and avoid making the same mistakes.

**disrespectful**—Not respectful

After the incident, when I'm not sure what to do, I observe other people and do things the way they do them. Even though this sometimes makes me feel that I am not being myself, it helps me avoid a lot of cultural difficulties. Of course, now I am also able to ask people questions. As I learn more, life here becomes much more interesting and enjoyable.

# Comprehension

**A.** *Tell whether these sentences are true or false.*

1. Yuan was confused when the students called the teacher "Miss White."

2. Yuan asked the students why they did this, but they would not tell her.

3. In Taiwan the respectful way to address teachers is to call them "Teacher."

4. Miss White was annoyed when Yuan called her "Teacher."

5. Yuan also felt very annoyed at Miss White.

6. Yuan discussed the misunderstanding with Miss White.

7. Yuan's uncle laughed at Yuan.

8. Yuan does not enjoy American culture anymore.

**B.** *Answer these questions.*

1. Why did Yuan think it was disrespectful to call her teacher "Miss White"?

2. Why did Miss White get mad at Yuan?

3. Why didn't Yuan ask her classmates about the problem?

4. What did Yuan's uncle tell her?

5. What does Yuan do now when she is not sure about what to do in a new situation?

**C.** *Give your opinion.*

1. Do you think the teacher treated Yuan in the right way? Why or why not?

2. Were you surprised when Yuan was angry and sad for a few days? Why or why not?

3. How would you have felt if Miss White had talked to you that way?

4. Do you think Yuan's uncle gave good advice? Why or why not?

5. Yuan now observes other people before she tries something new. Do you do the same? Are there other ways to avoid problems? What are these other ways?

UNIT 9   *Forms of Address*

**D.** *Now add your own ideas to the story.*

1. Does Miss White think Yuan is trying to be disrespectful when she calls her "Teacher"? Does Miss White think Yuan is not too smart? Does she think something else? Explain.

2. How does Miss White feel after Yuan explains the Chinese custom to her?

3. Does Yuan feel guilty about her mistake?

4. Does Miss White feel guilty about her treatment of Yuan?

5. Is Yuan's uncle sympathetic to her? Does he think that she is too sensitive or foolish? Or something else?

**E.** *Compare yourself with Yuan.*

1. What did Yuan learn?

2. What did you learn from Yuan's story?

# Vocabulary ||||➡

*Replace the underlined word(s) in the sentences with the words below.*

| | | | | |
|---|---|---|---|---|
| address | local | problems | upset | proper |
| interrupted | avoid | annoyed | observes | mistakes |

1. Miss White seemed slightly angry when Yuan asked questions.

2. While Yuan was speaking, Miss White talked out of turn.

3. Yuan had many difficulties with her English.

4. Yuan went to a nearby school.

5. Yuan tries to avert cultural difficulties.

6. Yuan watches the way other people do things.

7. Yuan's uncle taught her how not to make errors.

8. In Taiwan you say "Teacher" when you greet your teacher.

9. What is right in Taiwan is not necessarily polite in the United States.

10. Yuan wanted to know why Americans became agitated when she was only trying to be respectful.

# CULTURE CAPSULE

Children are called by their first names, but adults are often addressed by their last names with a title in front. The title "Mr." (mister) is used for men. The title "Miss" is used for single women. "Mrs." (pronounced "missus") is used for married women, and "Ms." (pronounced "miz") is used for single or married women. In school, students usually address their teachers by whichever of these titles is appropriate and their last name (Ms. Fontes). In college, however, teachers are often called by the special title "Professor" and their last name (Professor Dresser). Political figures are also addressed with special titles (Senator Wong, Mayor Garey), as are doctors (Dr. Diaz).

# Cultural Exchange

**A.** *Tell whether these sentences about the United States are true or false.*

1. "Ms." is used for both single and married women.

2. "Miss" is used for both single and married women.

3. In college, it is proper to call a teacher "Professor" before saying the last name.

4. If a senator is a woman, use the term "Mrs." before her last name.

5. "Mr." is the correct title for a man.

**B.** *Fill in the chart below, and then share your answers with your classmates.*

| In Your Country How Do People Address . . . | |
|---|---|
| A mother? | |
| A father? | |
| A grandfather? | |
| A sales clerk? | |
| A spouse? | |
| A mother-in-law? | |
| A boss? | |
| A college professor? | |
| A physician? | |
| A friend? | |

**spouse**—A person's husband or wife

**C.** *Discuss these questions with your classmates.*

1. In your culture, how are you addressed in a formal situation?

2. In your culture, how are you addressed by close friends?

3. Have you ever been addressed differently by someone from another culture? Describe what happened.

4. From what you have learned or seen in movies or on TV, do you think forms of address are more formal in the United States or in your culture? Can you give an example?

5. In your culture, when a woman gets married does she take her husband's name? What do you know about this custom in the United States?

6. What American names do you like?

7. If you were to move to the United States, would you choose an American name or keep your own, even if everyone had trouble pronouncing it? Explain.

# Expansion

*Work in small groups. Practice using forms of address and titles.*

1. Take three index cards and make business cards by writing your name on each of them in three different ways.

   a. On the first card print only your first and last name.

   b. On the second card add either Mr., Miss, Ms., or Mrs. in front of your name.

   c. On the third card give yourself a title before your name—for example, Doctor, Professor, Senator, Mayor, Governor, President, Vice President. Or put a title after your name. You can use Manager, Editor, Attorney-at-Law, Ph.D., D.D.S., or anything else you can think of. Note that when you use a title afterward, you need to add a comma after your name—for example, Betty Woolf, Publisher.

2. Now introduce yourself to a classmate and hand that person your card. You can say these words: "Hello, my name is _____. May I give you my card?" Then have the other person give you one of his or her cards while that person introduces himself or herself to you. Note: In the United States it is not necessary to use two hands to present a calling card or business card. Most Americans use one hand only.

3. When everyone has had a chance to exchange cards, discuss the following questions:

   a. How do you feel when you use just your first and last name?

   b. How do you feel when you have Mr. or Mrs. in front of your name?

   c. How do you feel when you have a professional title?

# Follow-Up

**A.** *Give a brief oral or written report. Tell about your own name. When you do, consider including the following details:*

> How was your name chosen?
>
> Who chose it?
>
> Were you named after anyone special?
>
> What is the meaning of your name?
>
> What is the history of your name?
>
> Do you like your name?
>
> Would you like to have someone named after you?
>
> If you could change your name, would you? If so, what would you change it to?

**B.** *In writing or aloud, retell Yuan's story from Miss White's point of view.*

# U N I T 10
# *Body Language*

## ? Do you know...

1. Do Americans usually look other people directly in the eye or avoid eye contact?

2. What are some gestures you have seen that are commonly used?

# An Eye for an Eye

*Read the story.*

My name is Lorena. I was born in Mexico and came to the United States when I was two. According to Mexican culture, when spoken to by an adult, children show respect by bowing their heads and not looking the adult directly in the eye. This way of showing respect caused me a problem when I went to school.

It was a sunny September morning, my first day at my new private school. The only person I knew was Tina, a girl from my Sunday school, and we sat next to each other and talked. The whole class was talking and giggling; everyone was happy to see old friends again.

Mrs. Georges asked us to be quiet. Then she passed out papers with addition and subtraction problems. Almost immediately, Tina asked me, "What did you get for number four?" I started to tell her, but Mrs. Georges called out, "Lorena, turn around and be quiet!" Just then, the school secretary came into the room with a message for Mrs. Georges. While they were busy speaking, Tina asked me another question. I turned to tell her to stop. Mrs. Georges must have seen me. She called out, "Lorena, come up here right now!"

My hands got moist. My heart beat fast. I took slow, short steps up to Mrs. Georges's desk. In a whisper I said, "Yes, Mrs. Georges?" I looked down at the floor. Mrs. Georges asked, "What were you doing?" I kept my head down and didn't say anything. Her voice got louder. "What were you doing?"

The next thing I knew, Mrs. Georges grabbed my arm tightly. "Look at me when I speak to you!" she said, and she made me look at her. I was scared because I had never before looked into the face of an adult who was speaking to me—not even my parents or grandparents.

For the rest of the day I felt very upset, and when I got home, I told my parents what happened. The next day, my mom went to school with me. We met with Mrs. Georges and explained that in our culture it was disrespectful to look an older person in the eye.

**giggling**—Laughing in a silly manner
**moist**—Slightly wet or damp

UNIT 10   *Body Language*

Mrs. Georges explained that in American culture it was disrespectful not to look someone in the eye. When I understood, I told Mrs. Georges that I was sorry. She said she was sorry too, and then she gave me a great big hug.

As a result of this experience I always try to look at anyone who is speaking. I'm a part of America because I live here. I have had to adapt, and now I tell my own child to look at me when I speak to her. I do not want her to experience what I did. That day in school, Mrs. Georges and I learned something about each other's culture. We learned the hard way, but it helped us both.

**adapt**—Change to fit into a new situation

# Comprehension

*A. Tell whether these sentences are true or false.*

1. In Mexico, children show respect for adults by looking them in the eye.

2. On her first day at her new school, Lorena did not know anyone in her classroom.

3. Lorena wanted Tina to give her an answer to a math problem.

4. Mrs. Georges got angry when she saw Lorena turning around to talk to Tina.

5. Lorena became scared when Mrs. Georges called her up to the desk.

6. Lorena had never before looked an adult in the eye while they were speaking.

7. Mrs. Georges apologized when she found out why Lorena would not look her in the eye.

*B. Answer these questions.*

1. What was Lorena taught to do when speaking to adults?

2. How did Lorena know Tina?

3. Why was Lorena about to talk to Tina?

4. How did Lorena feel when Mrs. Georges called her to the desk?

5. Why did Mrs. Georges become really angry and grab Lorena's arm?

6. What happened the next day?

**C.** *Give your opinion.*

1. What kind of person was Tina? Why do you think so?

2. How do you think Lorena felt about Tina after this incident? Why?

3. Do you think Mrs. Georges was a mean teacher or a nice one? Explain.

4. Why do you think Americans consider it disrespectful not to look a person in the eye?

5. Were you ever called up to the desk by an angry teacher, or did an angry teacher ever ask to see you after class? What happened?

**D.** *Now add your own ideas to the story.*

1. Why does Mrs. Georges think Lorena won't look at her?

2. Is Lorena afraid to tell her mother that she got into trouble with Mrs. Georges?

3. Is Lorena's mother angry with Mrs. Georges for upsetting her daughter? Is she angry with Lorena for getting into trouble?

4. Does Mrs. Georges change her attitude toward Lorena? If so, how?

5. Will Mrs. Georges change her classroom behavior in any way after this incident?

**E.** *Compare yourself with Lorena.*

1. What did Lorena learn?

2. What did you learn from Lorena's story?

# Vocabulary

*Replace the underlined word(s) in the sentences with the words below.*

| | | | | |
|---|---|---|---|---|
| sunny | adults | grabbed | directly | moist |
| immediately | adapt | tightly | giggling | message |

1. In the classroom the students were talking and <u>laughing</u>.

2. <u>Right away</u> Tina asked Lorena for the answer.

3. It was a <u>brightly lit</u> morning.

4. Mexican children don't look at adults <u>straight</u> in the eyes.

5. In Mexican culture children must show respect to <u>grown-ups</u>.

6. The school secretary brought a <u>note</u> for Mrs. Georges.

7. When Mrs. Georges called Lorena to come up to her desk, Lorena was so frightened her hands became <u>damp</u>.

8. Mrs. Georges was angry, and she <u>seized</u> Lorena's arm.

9. Mrs. Georges held Lorena's arm <u>securely</u>.

10. Lorena has had to <u>adjust</u> to American culture.

# CULTURE CAPSULE

We communicate not only with words but also with "body language" such as facial expressions, gestures, and movements. Like words, body language differs from culture to culture. In some cultures, for example, looking someone in the eye is disrespectful, but in the United States it is a way of showing you are being honest and truthful.

Gestures are the easiest part of body language to describe and learn. Some gestures are as common as words. Moving your head up and down means yes. Moving your head from side to side means no. Lifting your shoulders up and down means you don't know. You can say hello or goodbye by waving your hand up and down or from side to side.

Making a fist with the thumb extended downward is a sign of disapproval, called "thumbs down." Making a fist with the thumb extended upward is a sign of approval, "thumbs up." Another sign that means everything is all right, or "A-OK," is when the index finger joins the thumb to look like a big O.

**facial expression**—Eye, mouth, or nose movements that communicate a certain meaning

**gestures**—Movement, usually of the hands, to express a certain meaning

**fist**—The hand when tightly closed, with the fingers bent into the palm

# Cultural Exchange

**A.** *Tell whether these sentences about the United States are true or false.*

1. It is disrespectful to look someone in the eye.

2. Moving your head from side to side means yes.

3. Making a fist with the thumb extended downward is a sign of approval.

4. Waving your hand up and down or from side to side is a way to say goodbye.

5. Lifting your shoulders up and down means no.

**B.** *Fill in the chart below, and then share your answers with your classmates.*

| In Your Country What Gestures Do People Make for. . . | |
|---|---|
| Crazy? | |
| Be quiet? | |
| Goodbye? | |
| Go away? | |
| Come here? | |
| Yes? | |
| No? | |
| Stop? | |
| Wishing for luck? | |
| Delicious (food)? | |
| Everything is fine? | |
| I don't know? | |

***C.*** *Discuss these questions with your classmates.*

1. In your culture, what does a smile mean? When is it used? When is it never used?

2. From what you have learned or seen in movies or on TV, what does a smile mean in the United States?

3. In your country are gestures used more often than in the United States? Less often? About as often?

4. Are there any American gestures that you use? Which ones?

5. In your country, do people use their hands while speaking? Do they use their hands more often than Americans do, or less?

6. Do you know of any gestures that are the same in your country and the United States? Which ones? Do some gestures look the same but have different meanings?

7. Can you think of any facial expressions or other kinds of body language besides gestures that are used differently in your country than in the United States? What are they?

8. What gestures are you familiar with from countries other than the United States and your own?

# Expansion

*To increase your awareness of how people use body language, make observations outside the classroom.*

1. Observe two or three different conversations. If possible, observe conversations involving men and women, older and younger people, and those from your culture and outside your culture. Pay attention to people's body language. You might want to take notes. Try to notice the following:

   What gestures do people use?

   What other examples of body language do people use?

   How far apart do people stand while talking?

   Do people wait for the other person to finish talking or do they interrupt each other? Do people do about the same amount of talking?

   How much eye contact do people make?

2. Compare your observations with those made by your classmates. Were there differences in body language between men and women? Between people of your culture and other cultures? Between older and younger people? If so, what were these differences?

# Follow-Up ✓

**A.** *Give a brief oral or written report. Give an explanation of a gesture used in your own culture. In your report, consider including some of the following details:*

Describe the gesture.

What is its meaning?

When is it used? (when a person is angry? happy? sad? afraid?)

When did you first see it used?

Is it used more by men or by women? By children or by adults?

Do you use it often? Why or why not?

Is there an American gesture that has a similar meaning?

**B.** *On a sheet of paper illustrate a gesture either from your own culture or from American culture. Make the drawing large enough so the gesture can easily be seen. Ask your classmates if they know what it means. Ask your teacher to display the drawings, and compare the gestures you and your classmates have drawn.*

# UNIT 11
# *Touching in Public*

## ? Do you know...

1. Is it acceptable if two people hug or kiss in public?

2. In the United States, if two adults hold hands in public, are they friends or are they in love?

# I Want to Hold Your Hand

*Read the story.*

My name is May, and I came from Taiwan. Back there best friends always walk hand in hand because holding hands is our way of showing friendship. Now that I have been here for several years, I know that friends of the same sex, and even mothers and teenage daughters, seldom go hand in hand, but I didn't know that when I first came to America.

My first year in the United States, I met a girl who had been my classmate in Taiwan. We were excited that we had met again on the other side of the earth, and of course we became best friends. No one really knew about us being best friends because we weren't in the same class. Then one day we were walking hand in hand down the street to get some ice cream. A classmate saw us and seemed very surprised to see us like that. She told us that in the United States, if people walk hand in hand, other people will think they are lovers. Friends usually don't hold hands. After that, we never went hand in hand in public, but only when we were in our own houses or among Chinese people.

A few months later, my cousin visited me from Taiwan. She immediately noticed that I didn't walk hand in hand with her. She felt sad because she thought I didn't like her as I used to. I tried to explain, but she didn't understand. Finally, a few years later, I went back there for summer vacation. When I went out with my family or old friends shopping, to movies, or anywhere else, I walked hand in hand with them. My cousin was so happy that I liked her again. I told her that I always liked her and that I will explain everything to her when she grows up more. After all, it is hard for a person to understand or accept that other places have different cultures if he or she has never lived in a different place.

# Comprehension

**A.** *Tell whether these sentences are true or false.*

1. In Taiwan best friends always walk hand in hand.

2. In the United States best friends always walk hand in hand.

3. In the United States, mothers and teenage daughters usually walk hand in hand.

4. May still holds hands with her best friend in her own home.

5. When May would not hold her cousin's hand, the cousin thought May did not like her anymore.

6. May continued the custom of not holding hands when she visited Taiwan.

7. May's cousin is still angry with her.

**B.** *Answer these questions.*

1. In Taiwan how do two persons of the same sex show their friendship?

2. In the United States if two persons walk hand in hand, what might people think?

3. How did May find out about the American custom of not holding hands?

4. What did the cousin think when May did not walk hand in hand with her?

5. What did the cousin think when May returned to Taiwan and held hands with her again?

6. According to May, why was it hard for her cousin to understand?

**C.** *Give your opinion.*

1. Do you think it was a good idea that May's friend explained the custom of two girls not holding hands? Why or why not?

2. Do you think you would explain something like this to another classmate who was new to this culture? Why or why not?

3. Do you think May made the right choice in choosing not to hold hands with her friend? Explain your answer.

**D.** *Now add your own ideas to the story.*

1. How do May and her friend feel as they go to get ice cream?

2. What are they talking about?

3. How does the classmate feel telling them about the difference in hand-holding customs? How does the classmate go about telling them?

4. How do May and her friend react to what the classmate says?

5. How do they feel toward the classmate? Are they grateful, resentful, or something else?

*E. Compare yourself with May.*

1. What did May learn?

2. What did you learn from May's story?

# Vocabulary ‖‖‖▶

*Complete the sentences with the appropriate words. Circle the letter of the correct answer.*

1. In Taiwan walking hand in hand is a way to express _____.
   a. family relationships
   b. hatred
   c. friendship

2. In the United States even mothers and teenage daughters _____ walk hand in hand.
   a. seldom
   b. often
   c. always

3. May and her friend met again on the other side of the _____.
   a. earth
   b. street
   c. moon

4. When the classmate saw May and her friend walking hand in hand, she was very _____.
   a. pleased
   b. angry
   c. surprised

5. It is difficult for a person to understand or _____ that other places have different cultures.
   a. believe
   b. accept
   c. learn

6. May's cousin _____ that she didn't walk hand in hand with her.
   a. didn't see
   b. worried
   c. noticed

7. May plans to _____ everything to her cousin in a few more years.
   a. explain
   b. exorcise
   c. exclaim

# CULTURE CAPSULE

In the United States, unlike some cultures, lovers can walk down the street holding hands or with their arms around each other. They may even kiss in public and people usually won't mind. A husband and wife can also hold hands or kiss in public. On the other hand, although in many cultures friends walk hand in hand or with their arms around each other, friends in America rarely show affection in these ways.

# Cultural  Exchange

**A.** *Tell whether these sentences about the United States are true or false.*

1. A boyfriend and girlfriend can walk down the street holding hands.

2. A boyfriend and girlfriend cannot walk down the street with their arms around each other.

3. People get angry when they see a boy and girl kissing in public.

4. Husbands and wives may kiss in public.

5. Friends usually do not walk hand in hand.

**B.** *Discuss these questions with your classmates.*

1. In your culture, how do close friends express affection when in public? Are the customs for male friends different from those for female friends? Would these ways of expressing affection be acceptable in American culture?

2. In your culture, how do lovers express affection when in public?

3. In your culture, how do family members express affection when in public?

4. In your culture, are customs for a husband and wife expressing affection in public different from those for boyfriend and girlfriend? If so, in what ways?

5. What has surprised you about American customs of touching and displaying affection in public?

6. In general, do people who are romantically involved display affection in public more openly in your culture or in American culture? In general, do people who are close friends display affection in public more openly in your culture or in American culture?

7. In your culture, are any changes occurring in rules for touching in public?

# Expansion

*Work with a partner. Read the situations and decide which is the best answer for each question. Choose an answer for both your culture and American culture. You may have two answers. Then compare your answers with your classmates' answers.*

1. A husband and wife are out walking. They stop and give each other a hug and a kiss on the lips. What will people think?
   a. It is a sign of bad taste.
   b. It is a sign that they love each other.
   c. It is a sign that the husband disrespects his wife.

2. An unmarried man and woman are on a first date. They are waiting in line for a movie and the man pats the woman's behind. What will people think?
   a. The woman should be offended.
   b. She should slap his face.
   c. It is acceptable.

3. At a family wedding a married man asks his unmarried sister-in-law to dance. What will people think?
   a. He disrespects his wife.
   b. It is acceptable.
   c. It is not acceptable.

4. A man and woman in their late seventies are sitting on a park bench. The man gives the woman a passionate kiss. What will people think?
   a. People will smile.
   b. People will be disgusted.
   c. The man and woman should be ashamed.

5. A married man meets in a restaurant a woman friend who is also married. They give each other a kiss on the cheek. What will people think?
   a. They have low morals.
   b. It is acceptable.
   c. Their husband and wife will be angry.

6. A twelve-year-old boy and girl are kissing and walking with their arms around each other. What will people think?
   a. The girl will be considered a "bad" girl.
   b. It is acceptable.
   c. Their parents will not approve.

# Follow-Up

*A. Give a brief oral or written report. Choose number 1 or 2.*

1. Tell about a time when someone else's public behavior made you feel uncomfortable.

2. Tell about a time when your own public behavior was very different from the behavior of those around you.

*In your report, consider including some of the following details:*

When did the incident take place?

Where were you living at the time?

Who was involved?

What was their relationship to each other?

What was the behavior that was different or that caused you to be uncomfortable?

What did the behavior mean to you?

How did you react?

How did others react?

As a result of this incident, did anyone change his or her behavior or attitudes?

*B. You are a writer for a magazine in your country. Your assignment is to write an article describing American attitudes about touching in public and other public behavior. In the article, compare American customs with those in your country.*

# U n i t 12
# *Dating*

## ? Do you know…

1. At what age do young people in the United States begin dating?

2. If a couple is dating, does this mean that they plan to get married?

# Breaking Up

*Read the story.*

I am a Chinese girl from Vietnam, and my name is Nancy. My parents, who are very strict, did not let me date until I was eighteen. My first boyfriend was an American guy named Ian. Although my parents were opposed to my seeing him, they learned to accept it because they wanted me to be happy. One day I invited Ian over to my house for dinner so that my parents could meet him. Unfortunately, that invitation led to the end of my relationship with Ian.

According to Chinese custom, the guy a girl is dating is expected to be her future husband. I have been exposed to the American concept that girls can date any guy they want and not have to worry about making commitments. Since my parents are very old-fashioned, we sometimes had arguments about dating. Because of these arguments, I should have realized what my parents would do when Ian came to my house. But I didn't. And Ian only expected to have a nice relaxing dinner with my family.

This "relaxing" dinner became a disastrous dinner when my parents, especially my mom, started asking Ian questions. And I was the one who had to translate these questions. They asked him what his future goals were, what his parents' occupations were, how many brothers and sisters he had, and even what his educational and financial background was. I was shocked that my parents actually asked those questions. Ian was more than shocked—he was obviously stunned. Fortunately, he was very polite and respectful to my parents and suffered through the night. When it was time for Ian to go home, I could tell from the expression on his face that he was glad to be going.

Obviously, Ian noticed that my parents were expecting him to be my future husband. But Ian is an American guy and American guys tend to date a lot before they are ready to settle down. He told me that it was the first time he had ever gone to a girlfriend's house for dinner where he had to answer so many

**breaking up**—Ending a dating relationship

**dating**—Going out socially with someone of the opposite sex

**to be exposed**—To learn about

**commitments**—Promises to be with one person only

**stunned**—Very shocked or surprised

**tend to**—To be likely to behave in a certain way

questions about himself and his family. We decided that, because of our different cultural backgrounds, we would just be friends from then on. I believe we made the right decision.

# Comprehension

**A.** *Tell whether these sentences are true or false.*

1. Nancy's parents were opposed to her dating Ian but learned to accept it.

2. Nancy's parents learned to accept the American concept that a girl can date without making a commitment to marry.

3. Ian knew when he started dating Nancy that he was expected to marry her.

4. The dinner table conversation was all in English.

5. Both Nancy and Ian had a good time.

6. Ian was rude to Nancy's parents.

7. Nancy and Ian are now engaged.

**B.** *Answer these questions.*

1. According to Chinese tradition, what does it mean when a girl and a boy are dating?

2. Why did Nancy's parents let her date Ian even though they were opposed to it?

3. What kinds of questions did Nancy's mom ask Ian?

4. How did Nancy react to these questions?

5. How did Ian react to these questions?

6. What happened to Nancy and Ian's relationship?

**C.** *Give your opinion.*

1. Do you think Nancy's parents made the right decision to allow her to date someone from another culture? Why or why not?

2. Why do you think Nancy did not try to stop her mother from questioning Ian?

3. Do you think Ian behaved properly at the table? Is there anything he could have done differently to improve the situation?

4. If you had been Nancy, what would you have done to ease the tension at the dinner table?

5. Do you think Nancy and Ian made the right decision to just be friends? Explain your answer.

**D.** *Now add your own ideas to the story.*

1. Is Nancy embarrassed or angry with her mom?

2. Does Nancy feel guilty about putting Ian into this situation?

3. Is the mother angry with Nancy for picking a non-Chinese boyfriend?

4. Is Ian understanding of Nancy's problem, or is he angry with her?

5. Is Nancy's mother sorry about the evening or happy that her daughter is finished with Ian?

**E.** *Compare yourself with Nancy.*

1. What did Nancy learn?

2. What did you learn from Nancy's story?

# Vocabulary ▐▐▐▶

*Complete the sentences with the appropriate words. Circle the letter of the correct answer.*

1. Nancy's parents were opposed to her dating Ian; that means _____.
   a. they were against her dating Ian
   b. they were happy about her dating Ian

2. When Nancy ended her relationship with Ian, _____.
   a. she stopped seeing him anymore
   b. she stopped going to school

3. When Nancy writes about the American concept of dating, she is referring to _____.
   a. printed stories about dating
   b. the ideas and rules of dating

4. Nancy had arguments with her mother about dating, which means that _____.
   a. they agreed about dating
   b. they disagreed about dating

5. Nancy's mother asked Ian about his parents' occupations. She wanted to know _____.
   a. what kinds of jobs they had
   b. what kinds of leisure activities they enjoyed

6. Someone's financial background tells about _____.
   a. what kind of furniture they have at home
   b. how much money they have

*Continued on the following page*

7. Nancy's mother wanted to know about Ian's "goals," another word for _____.

    a. ambitions

    b. golf

8. Nancy believes she and Ian made the right decision, which refers to _____.

    a. making a judgment about their situation

    b. making a mistake

9. One day Nancy will settle down with someone else. She will _____.

    a. get married

    b. get a permanent job

10. Ian had looked forward to a nice relaxing dinner with Nancy and her family. He expected it to be _____.

    a. easygoing and informal

    b. formal

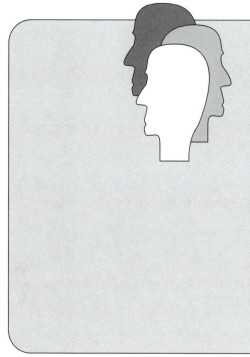

# CULTURE CAPSULE

Some boys and girls may start dating, or "going out," as early as thirteen or fourteen years old. That means they will go somewhere alone or with other friends without any adults along. Later, when they can drive (about sixteen or seventeen), it is acceptable for a boy and a girl to go out together in a car. Dating does not mean that the boy and girl will get married. On the contrary, people think it is a good idea for young adults to go out with different members of the opposite sex. That way they will meet different kinds of people and learn what kind of person they really want to marry.

Some couples who are in their twenties or older may share an apartment and "live together" before they get married. They think this helps to see whether a marriage might work. But many parents are still opposed to young people living together before marriage.

# Cultural ⮕ ⬅ Exchange

**A.** *Tell whether these sentences about the United States are true or false.*

1. Boys and girls can drive at fourteen.

2. Dating does not mean that the boy and girl will get married.

3. Americans are opposed to dating.

4. Most parents are happy when their children live together with someone of the opposite sex before they are married.

5. It is acceptable for a boy and girl to go out together in a car without an accompanying adult.

**B.** *Fill in the chart below, and then share your answers with your classmates.*

| When It Comes to Dating in Your Country . . . | |
|---|---|
| Can an unmarried man and woman go out alone together? Beginning at what age? | |
| Can a man visit a woman's home without their being engaged? | |
| Can a woman date someone other than the man she will marry? | |
| Must parents approve of their daughter's date? | |
| How do young adults find marriage partners? (through friends? family? dating services? advertisements? other?) | |
| What is the usual age difference for an engaged couple? | |
| What is a typical age at which women marry? What is a typical age for men? | |

*C. Discuss these questions with your classmates.*

1. In your country, what happens when a person wants to date someone from a different culture? Does this cause problems, or is it acceptable? Explain.

2. In your country, do people ever go on blind dates?

3. In your country, what would be a typical date for a couple in their twenties? (going out to eat? dancing? movie? walking? other?)

4. From what you have learned or seen in movies or on TV, how would a typical date in your country be similar to a typical date in the United States? How would it differ?

**blind date**—Going out with someone you have never met before

5. What part of American dating customs do you like?

6. What part of American dating customs do you not like?

# Expansion

*Many American newspapers have advice columns that answer letters from people asking for advice on love problems or other problems. With a partner, write a letter asking for advice about a problem relating to life in American culture. Switch letters with another pair of students. Write each other a letter giving advice. Share these problems and solutions with the whole class. You can choose a problem from the list on page 91, adding more information, or you can make up your own problem.*

*Here is a sample letter:*

```
Dear Broken Hearts Club:

I am a twenty-five-year-old single woman who works in a bank.
I am very happy with my job. I like going out on weekends with
my co-workers. We go shopping, to the movies, and eat out. My
problem is that I am the only one of my brothers and sisters
who is not married. My parents are very unhappy about this.
They believe that all women should get married and have
children, but I am not interested. I would rather just have
a career. And now the bank is offering me a promotion.

My parents are against this. They want me to marry a friend
of theirs—an older businessman. He would like that too, but I
just don't care for him at all. My parents are pressuring me
into a marriage with this man and I am torn between pleasing
my parents and pleasing myself. What should I do?
```

*Here are some other problems:*

**Dear Broken Hearts Club:**

1. My boyfriend and I want to get married, but my family hates his long hair.

2. I don't know how to meet young women even though I am handsome.

3. Men are just interested in me for my looks; they don't take me seriously as a person.

4. I love my boyfriend, but I don't know how to tell him he needs to take showers more often.

5. I have fallen in love with the man engaged to my sister, and I think he loves me too.

6. My wife would rather spend time with her friends than with me.

7. My girlfriend is wonderful, but I've heard that she flirts with other guys behind my back.

8. I love my girlfriend, but she has a three-year-old son who she brings on all our dates.

9. My boyfriend has a bad temper, and when we go out I get embarrassed by how he's always yelling at waiters, salespeople, and everyone else.

10. I'm dating a woman from another culture, and when her family gets together they don't speak my language.

# Follow-Up

**A.** *Give a brief oral or written report. Tell about the dating customs in your culture. In your report, consider including some of the following details:*

How old are young men and women when they begin to date?

Can you date a variety of people or only your future husband/wife?

What are some ways you can meet people to date?

Where do you go on dates?

Do other people accompany you?

Must you be home by a certain hour?

Does the man pay for all expenses?

Does the man ever give gifts to the woman? Does the woman ever give gifts to the man? What kinds of gifts are given?

What are the advantages and disadvantages of your dating customs compared with American dating customs?

**B.** *In the United States, some people find a boyfriend or girlfriend by advertising in newspapers or magazines. Sometimes they may even go to a computerized dating service.*

*Pretend that you are unmarried and are looking for someone to date and eventually marry. Fill in the blanks of the questionnaire to help you find the man or woman of your dreams.*

I am looking for the _____ of my dreams. _____ should be
                    (man or woman)                 (He or She)

about _____ tall and weigh about _____. This person should
         (height)                   (weight)

have _____ hair and _____ eyes, and I want someone who
        (color)            (color)

likes to _____ and is also interested in _____.
      (hobby or sport)              (another interest)

I hope this person likes to listen to _____ music and likes to eat
                       (favorite music)

_____ because these are my favorites. I hope I can find my ideal mate,
(favorite food)

who has a _____ personality and one who also
          (describe)

_____.
(finish on your own)

# UNIT 13

# *Weddings*

## ? Do you know...

**1.** What is the traditional color for wedding gowns?

**2.** What do the maid of honor and the best man do at a wedding?

# Lady in Red

*Read the story.*

I'm from China, and my name is Su. The problem I will tell about began one day when I was sitting with friends at lunchtime talking and laughing. My friend Jan told the rest of us that we were invited to her sister's wedding. I was very excited because I had never been to an American wedding. Her sister's wedding was going to be held the following week.

When school was over, I rushed home so excited that I forgot to take my algebra book. I was thinking of what to wear to the wedding. I thought of wearing black and white but then decided that would not be appropriate for a wedding. Well, I sat in my room thinking for hours and still I couldn't come up with anything. Then, looking around my room, I noticed something red and thought, why not wear all red to the wedding?

I asked my mother her opinion and she told me that red would be a good color, that in China the color red was for good luck. The next day she went shopping with me. We couldn't find anything for several hours. Finally, I found a red suit that I thought was fabulous. It was made out of silk; the pants were very baggy, and the blouse was like a jacket with see-through sleeves. Next, I went to buy a pair of shoes. I bought a white pair with cute red bows on the front.

The day of the wedding my friends picked me up so that we could go together to Jan's house. I was the only one who was wearing red. When we got to Jan's house, she greeted us and gave me this funny look, which I didn't like. She seemed mad, but I didn't know why. When she introduced us to her family, her family also gave me this funny look I didn't like. After that, Jan and her family never spoke to me once the whole day. I wanted to cry because everyone kept looking at me like I had done something wrong.

Finally, the wedding was over. I got home and told my mom what happened. The next day, Jan called me and said we couldn't be friends anymore, but she didn't give me a reason. Later on, one of my friends told me that in Jan's religion the color red represents the devil. To Jan and her family my red dress was disrespectful and a sign of bad luck. They thought that by wearing red I was putting the wedding couple in danger. My friend also told me that at most American weddings the red suit would not have been a problem at all. I found all this confusing, but at least I finally understood what had happened.

In conclusion, I think that people shouldn't stop being friends or get angry at other people if they do something wrong just because of a cultural misunderstanding. I think people should talk things over before ending their friendship.

# Comprehension

*A.* *Tell whether these sentences are true or false.*

1. Su's friend Jan was getting married.

2. Su had been to other American weddings.

3. Su did not think she should wear black and white to a wedding.

4. Su's mother did not think she should wear red.

5. Su spent a lot of time shopping for her outfit.

6. Jan was happy to see Su when she arrived at the wedding.

7. Because of their religious beliefs, the family of the bride was offended by Su's clothes.

8. After the wedding Jan explained to Su why they could not be friends anymore.

*B.* *Answer these questions.*

1. Why did Su forget to bring her algebra book home?

2. What did Su's mother say about wearing red?

3. What did Su buy to wear to the wedding?

4. How did Jan and her family respond to Su at the wedding?

5. Why was the family offended?

### C. Give your opinion.

1. Do you think that Jan should have told people not to wear red? Why or why not?

2. Do you think Jan's family should have been more understanding about Su's mistake?

3. How do you think the bride and groom felt when they saw Su?

4. Do you think Jan should have explained to Su why they could not be friends? Why or why not?

5. Do you think there is some way that this incident could have turned out to be more positive? Explain your answer.

### D. Now add your own ideas to the story.

1. At the wedding, is Su angry, embarrassed, unhappy, or just puzzled?

2. Are Jan's parents angry with her for inviting Su?

3. Does Jan realize that Su just made a mistake? Will she ever forgive her?

4. How does Su react to Jan's explanation?

### E. Compare yourself with Su.

1. What did Su learn?

2. What did you learn from Su's story?

# Vocabulary

*Complete the sentences with one of the following words.*

| algebra | appropriate | religion | opinion |
|---------|-------------|----------|---------|
| fabulous | baggy | cute | danger |

1. Su left her _____ book at school.

2. She found some pants that were _____.

3. Jan's family belonged to a _____ that believed red was a bad-luck color.

4. Su wanted to wear colors that would be _____ for a wedding.

5. Su's mother gave her _____ about what Su should wear to the wedding.

6. Su purchased a _____ red silk suit.

7. She also bought shoes with _____ red bows on the front.

8. By wearing red, Su unknowingly put the wedding couple in _____.

# CULTURE CAPSULE

At a traditional wedding, the bride wears a long, fancy white dress and a veil and the groom wears a tuxedo. Friends and family of the bride and groom take part in the ceremony. The bride chooses a maid of honor to help her during the ceremony and bridesmaids who also walk down the aisle. Generally, the maid of honor and the bridesmaids wear matching dresses. The best man helps the groom during the ceremony. He and the other male assistants, called ushers, all wear tuxedos, or formal suits. Other wedding guests often wear their nicest clothing. There are no rules, though, except that females generally do not wear white, to avoid competing with the bride.

Different ethnic and religious groups have their own customs for weddings, including customs about what to wear. Also, many couples decide not to have traditional weddings, preferring wedding ceremonies that are less formal.

**veil**—Covering of net or fine cloth for the head or face

**tuxedo**—A man's formal evening suit, usually black

**maid of honor**—The principal bridesmaid who helps the bride

**bridesmaids**—Women, often unmarried, who help the bride on the day of the marriage ceremony

**aisle**—A space to walk through or between sections of seats as in a church or theater

**competing**—Trying to look or to do better than someone else

**ethnic**—Cultural, religious, national, or racial group

# Cultural Exchange

**A.** *Tell whether these sentences about the United States are true or false.*

1. The groom usually wears a tuxedo.

2. The maid of honor helps the bride.

3. Bridesmaids generally wear matching dresses.

4. Female guests usually don't wear white.

5. The men who assist the groom are called ushers.

*B. Fill in the chart, and then share your answers with your classmates.*

| At a Wedding in Your Country . . . | |
|---|---|
| What does the bride wear? | |
| What does the groom wear? | |
| Who pays for the wedding? | |
| What kinds of food and beverages are served? | |
| Is there music and dancing? | |
| Are there colors that guests should not wear? | |

*C. Discuss these questions with your classmates.*

1. In your culture, do the parents of either the bride or the groom give them money? Explain. Do they give them something else instead? Explain.

2. In your culture, when do friends and relatives give gifts to the bride and groom? What kinds of gifts are given?

3. In your culture, do married women wear a ring? On what finger? Do married men wear a ring? On what finger?

4. In your culture, does the newly married couple go on a brief holiday together following the wedding ceremony? Explain.

5. In your culture, do the newlyweds live on their own, or do they live with either the bride's family or the groom's family? If they live on their own, who furnishes the new home?

6. From what you have learned or seen in movies or on TV, what do you know about American weddings? How are they similar to or different from weddings in your culture?

7. Does anything about American wedding customs surprise you? Explain. Is there anything you particularly like or dislike?

8. If you are married, what kind of wedding did you have? If not, what kind of wedding would you like to have?

# Expansion

*To increase your vocabulary about wedding customs, solve this crossword puzzle with words from the list below.*

best man    garter    maid of honor    stag

bouquet    gifts    reception    thank-you

bride    groom    rice    trousseau

bridesmaids    honeymoon    ring    ushers

cake    I do    shower    veil

fun

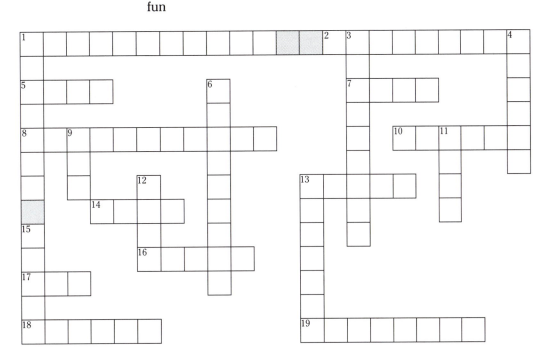

## Across

1. Female attendants of the bride
2. Personal items the bride-to-be accumulates before the wedding
5. All-male party given for the groom before the wedding: _____ party
7. Dessert served at all wedding parties
8. Female attendant who stands next to the bride
10. Sometimes worn by the bride around her leg
13. The woman who is getting married
14. Worn over the bride's face before the ceremony
16. The man who is getting married
17. What guests at the wedding party are expected to have
18. Party given for the bride before the wedding: bridal _____
19. Notes written by the bride after receiving wedding gifts: _____ _____ notes

## Down

1. Male attendant who hands groom the ring
3. Party given after the wedding ceremony
4. Male attendants at a wedding
6. Holiday the newlyweds take following the wedding
9. Words spoken during the ceremony
11. Thrown at the bride and groom as they leave the place where they were married
12. Placed on the bride's finger
13. Bride throws this to the unmarried women—whoever catches it will be the next one married
15. Given to the bride and groom by friends and family

# Follow-Up ✓

**A.** *Give a brief oral or written report. Choose number 1 or 2.*

1. Describe a wedding ceremony you attended that was from your own cultural tradition.

2. Describe a wedding ceremony you attended that was different from weddings in your own culture.

*In your report, consider including some of the following details:*

When did this wedding take place?

Where did the wedding take place?

What was the cultural background of the bride and groom?

How was the bride dressed?

Did she have attendants? Who were they? How were they dressed?

How was the groom dressed?

Did he have attendants? Who were they? How were they dressed?

Did the parents of the bride and groom do anything special during the ceremony?

Was there any kind of party after the ceremony? (music? food? dancing?)

Did anything unusual take place? Describe.

Did you have a good time? Why or why not?

**B.** *With a partner, make a list of household items you think every newly married couple needs. Compare your list with classmates' lists. What items are mentioned most often?*

# UNIT 14

# *Good Luck and Bad Luck*

## ? Do you know…

1. What do Americans consider to be lucky?
2. What do Americans consider to be unlucky?

# Debby's Birthday Present

*Read the story.*

My name is Debby. I was born in China and lived for many years in Hong Kong. When my family moved to the United States, there were many things that we were not used to. We worked hard to learn and accept the American life-style and culture. Making changes was especially difficult for my grandparents. They believe that Chinese people should follow Chinese customs no matter where they are.

Three years ago I met a girl named Reyna. She is Hispanic-American and has lived in the United States all her life. We became good friends almost right away. She taught me how to eat Mexican food, and I taught her how to use chopsticks. She told me about Mexican culture, and I told her about Chinese celebrations like the celebration of the full moon. On my sixteenth birthday, I invited Reyna to my house to have dinner with my family. My grandmother had made all of my favorite Chinese foods. When Reyna came to the house, she handed me a birthday gift. My family liked Reyna very much. We had a very nice dinner together, and after dinner we decided to open my gifts. Since I was eager to know what Reyna gave me, I opened her gift first. It was a black and white clock.

When my grandparents saw the clock, the expressions on their faces changed instantly. They became very angry and left the living room. Reyna didn't understand what was happening. I explained that getting a clock as a gift is bad luck, and to Chinese people, black and white objects are also bad luck. So, to my grandparents, the gift that Reyna gave me meant double bad luck on my birthday. I also told Reyna that another meaning of a clock is the end of life. After she heard my explanation of the meaning of her gift, she felt very bad. She didn't know what to do.

When Reyna left, my grandparents told me that I should not be her friend anymore, since she had wished me death on my birthday. I tried to explain that American people do not have that belief, but my grandparents wouldn't accept my explanation.

The next day, Reyna came to my house again. My grandparents were very rude to her. She gave me a bright red box and said, "Happy Birthday." I was surprised that she was not angry at the way my grandparents treated her. I opened the red box. Inside was a bright red dress. I tried it on, and it looked great on me. I showed it to my grandparents and told them it was from Reyna. They smiled at me and Reyna and told her they liked it very much.

As a result of this incident, I learned that Reyna was very understanding and a great friend to have. Obviously, Reyna learned never to give clocks or black and white gifts to Chinese people.

**rude**—Not polite; discourteous

# Comprehension

*A. Tell whether these sentences are true or false.*

1. Debby's grandparents did not want to adapt to American culture.

2. Reyna taught Debby about Mexican culture.

3. As soon as Debby's family saw Reyna, they did not like her.

4. In Chinese culture, a clock can mean death.

5. In Chinese culture, black and white means good luck.

6. Reyna felt bad about what she did.

7. When Reyna brought over the red dress in the red box, Debby was very happy.

8. Debby's grandparents never forgave Reyna.

*B. Answer these questions.*

1. Why were the grandparents offended when they saw the gift from Reyna?

2. What did the grandparents want Debby to do about her friendship with Reyna?

3. What did Reyna do to try to make up for her cultural mistake?

4. How did the grandparents react to the gift in the red box?

5. What did Reyna learn from this experience?

*C. Give your opinion.*

1. Why do you think it was hard for Debby's grandparents to accept the American life-style and culture?

2. Do you think Debby is close with her grandparents? Explain.

*Continued on the following page*

3. Do you think Debby's grandparents should have been kinder about the clock? Why do you think they weren't kinder?

4. Why did Reyna bring over a red dress in a red box?

5. What does this tell you about Reyna? Would you want her for your friend? Why?

**D.** *Now add your own ideas to the story.*

1. How do the grandparents feel when they think a stranger wishes death to Debby?

2. Does Debby feel torn between loyalty to her family and to her friend? Explain.

3. What does Reyna think when she discovers her mistake? How does this make her feel?

4. In the end, what do the grandparents think about Reyna?

5. How will this event affect Reyna's relationship with Debby?

**E.** *Compare yourself with Debby.*

1. What did Debby learn?

2. What did you learn from Debby's story?

# Vocabulary ‖‖‖➡

*Complete the sentences with the following words.*

| treated | customs | expressions | eager |
| celebrations | rude | instantly | life-style |

1. When Reyna returned the next day, Debby's grandparents were very _____ to her.

2. Debby's family believed that they should follow their Chinese _____ even though they were working hard to learn and accept the American _____ .

3. Debby's grandparents' faces changed _____ when they saw that Reyna had given Debby a clock.

4. Debby and Reyna taught one another about their own cultural _____ .

5. Debby was _____ to know what was inside Reyna's gift.

6. Debby was relieved when Reyna wasn't angry at the way her grandparents _____ her.

7. Debby could tell her grandparents were angry by the _____ on their faces.

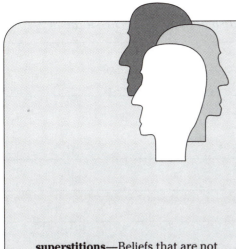

# CULTURE CAPSULE

Thirteen is thought to be an unlucky number. Most hotels do not have a thirteenth floor or a room number thirteen because people might not stay there. Friday the thirteenth is thought to be an unlucky day. Many people do not want to do anything dangerous, like have surgery, on Friday the thirteenth, and some do not even like to leave their houses. Some people believe that bad luck can come if a black cat crosses their path or if they open an umbrella inside the house, walk under a ladder, or break a mirror. There are also many superstitions about good luck. Some people think they will have good luck if they find a four-leaf clover, hang a horseshoe over their door, or wear a rabbit's foot.

**superstitions**—Beliefs that are not based on reason but are based on magic or old ideas

# Cultural Exchange

*A. Tell whether these sentences about the United States are true or false.*

1. Thirteen is an unlucky number.

2. Friday the thirteenth is a lucky day.

3. Black cats are lucky.

4. Four-leaf clovers are lucky.

5. Rabbits' feet are unlucky.

**B.** *Fill in the chart, and then share your answers with your classmates.*

| According to Superstition in Your Country, What Are Some . . . | |
|---|---|
| Good-luck charms to wear or carry? To hang in your home or car? | |
| Good-luck numbers? | |
| Bad-luck numbers? | |
| Bad-luck omens? (black cat? broken mirror? full moon? spilled salt? other?) | |
| Good-luck omens? (falling star? other?) | |
| Good-luck colors? | |
| Bad-luck colors? | |

**C.** *Discuss these questions with your classmates.*

1. In your culture, are there some things that you would never do because they might bring bad luck? (compliment a baby? open an umbrella inside the house? tell about something good before it happens? other?) Describe.

2. In your culture, is there anything you do to protect yourself from bad luck? (cross yourself? knock on wood? spit three times? cross your fingers? other?) Describe.

3. Are there things from your culture that some family members do that you do not do because you consider them too superstitious? Describe.

4. According to your culture, are there any things that you can do to change bad luck to good luck? (sprinkle something around the house? consult a special person? make an offering? other?) Describe.

5. Do you find that many American superstitions are the same as superstitions in your country? Are there any American superstitions that have surprised you?

# Expansion

*Interview at least two people outside of class and ask them if they know anything about the American superstitions listed below. Ask them if they know these superstitions, and if they practice or believe them. Do they have something similar? Bring your answers back to class and compare them with your classmates' answers.*

1. If you spill salt, you will have bad luck.

2. If you leave a hat on the bed, you will have bad luck.

3. If you see a falling star, you will have good luck.

4. If you knock on wood, it will keep bad luck from happening.

5. If you blow out all the candles on the birthday cake, you will have good luck.

6. If you see an owl flying or hear it hooting in the daytime, you will have bad luck.

7. If your palm itches, you will receive money.

8. If the groom sees the bride in her wedding dress before the ceremony, it is a sign of bad luck.

9. If a ladybug lands on you, you will have good luck.

10. If you find a coin and pick it up, you will have good luck.

# Follow-Up

*A. Give a brief oral or written report. Choose number 1 or 2.*

1. Tell about a time when you gave someone a gift that brought an unexpected reaction.

2. Tell about an experience when you had either good or bad luck.

*If you choose number 1, consider including some of the following details:*

When did this incident occur? Where were you living at the time?

What was the occasion for the gift?

Whom were you giving it to? What was the gift?

What response did you expect? What response did you receive?

How did it affect your relationship with the person?

What did you learn from this experience?

*Continued on the following page*

*If you choose number 2, consider including some of the following details:*

When did this incident occur?

Where were you living at the time?

Did you have good luck or bad luck?

What caused it?

What happened as a result of the good luck or bad luck?

What did you learn from the experience?

Has this bad luck or good luck occurred again since that time?

**B.** *Using an encyclopedia, work alone or with a partner and look up two of the following words. Write down their meanings and compare your answers with your classmates' answers. What do these words have in common? Which of these things exist in your culture?*

| | | |
|---|---|---|
| amulet | fortune-telling | oracles |
| astrology | ghost | Ouija board |
| dowsing | graphology | palmistry |
| evil eye | omens | seance |

# U N I T 15

# *Parents and Children*

## ? Do you know…

**1.** At what age is it acceptable for children to move out of their parents' home?

**2.** How are children usually punished?

# Respect

*Read the story.*

My name is Lily, and I was raised in a very conservative family on the island of Fiji, in the South Pacific. At an early age we were taught close family ties and conservative ways. Family members worked together as one unit, and we respected our elders. Upon arriving in the United States, I discovered a very different world, where children speak as they wish to their parents and at times even treat them with disrespect. This different world eventually led to some difficulties between me and my parents.

When I was eighteen, a couple of my friends moved out of their parents' house and into an apartment of their own. They asked me to move in with them. These friends were born in the United States, and their upbringing was less conservative than mine. Their parents considered it perfectly acceptable for them to move out and live independently at eighteen. But when I spoke to my parents, it was clear they did not want me to leave home. My friends couldn't understand this and they kept telling me to move out anyway. I felt caught between my friends and my parents. I felt that my friends were doing something that was socially acceptable and "in with the crowd" and that my parents were being old-fashioned and not behaving as Americans should behave.

For me, after many sleepless nights, my obligation as a daughter overcame my yearning for independence. I realized that my parents' unwillingness for me to move out was because of their love for me. I also realized that if my friends were true friends they would accept my decision. I told them I'd decided to stay with my parents. Some of my friends and I grew apart from each other but most of my friends accepted my decision. They realized that it did not matter whether I lived with my parents, that what really mattered for our friendship was how I was with them. Now, looking back, I feel that an eighteen-year-old is still young enough to make many mistakes, and I feel lucky that I didn't make a mistake.

**elders**—Older persons

**upbringing**—Training and education during childhood

**obligation**—One's duty

**yearning**—Having strong desire or great longing

# Comprehension

**A.** *Tell whether these sentences are true or false.*

1. Lily grew up in the United States.

2. Lily thinks that American children are sometimes disrespectful to their parents.

3. Lily's friends wanted her to move into an apartment with them.

4. Lily's parents encouraged her to move out.

5. Lily was torn between independence and obedience.

6. Lily decided to move out.

7. Lily now regrets the decision she made.

8. Lily lost some friends as a result of her decision.

**B.** *Answer these questions.*

1. What did Lily learn when she was growing up in Fiji?

2. What did Lily's friends want her to do?

3. Why was it acceptable for Lily's friends to move out?

4. Why didn't Lily's parents want her to move out?

5. Looking back, what does Lily now realize?

6. What happened to Lily's friendships as a result of her decision?

**C.** *Give your opinion.*

1. What do you think about the idea of children living on their own at age eighteen?

2. Do you think Lily made the right decision? Explain.

3. What kind of person is Lily? How do you know this?

4. What do you think about the way Lily's friends reacted to her decision? If you were a friend of Lily's would her decision affect your friendship?

5. Were you ever in a situation where your friends felt one way and your parents felt another way? What did you do?

**D.** *Now add your own ideas to the story.*

1. Is Lily afraid to say no to her friends? Is Lily afraid to tell her parents that she wants to move away from them?

2. How does Lily's mother feel about Lily being friends with people who have different values?

3. What do Lily's friends think when she says no? Are they disappointed, angry, or something else?

4. In the end, how does Lily feel? Is she disappointed or satisfied?

5. How will Lily's decision affect her friendships with the other people?

***E.** Compare yourself with Lily.*

1. What did Lily learn?

2. What did you learn from Lily's story?

# Vocabulary ▐▐▐▶

*What is the meaning of the underlined word or phrase?  Circle the letter of the correct answer.*

1. We were taught conservative ways.
   a. We learned how to save things.
   b. We learned to act in moderation.

2. At eighteen they were allowed to live independently.
   a. At eighteen they could live alone without their parents.
   b. At eighteen they could live intelligently.

3. Lily's obligations as a daughter came first.
   a. Lily's duty to take care of herself came first.
   b. Lily's duty to her parents came first.

4. She yearned for independence.
   a. She wanted so much to be on her own.
   b. She wanted so much to be taken care of by her parents.

5. Her parents were unwilling for Lily to move out.
   a. Lily's parents wanted her to stay at home.
   b. Lily's parents didn't want her to stay at home.

6. Their parents considered it acceptable for them to move out of the house and into their own apartment.
   a. Their parents were against their moving into their own apartment.
   b. Their parents thought it was all right for them to move into their own apartment.

7. Our differences eventually led to some difficulties.
   a. Our differences never led to any problems.
   b. Our differences finally led to some problems.

8. I felt caught between my friends and my parents.
   a. I felt trapped.
   b. I felt happy.

9. We worked together as one unit.
   a. We worked independently.
   b. We were unified.

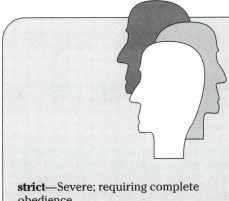

# CULTURE CAPSULE

Generally, American parents want their children to become independent. Therefore, they often encourage their children to make their own decisions, give their own opinions, and get jobs outside the home. It is also generally acceptable for children over eighteen to move out and get their own apartments, especially since eighteen is the usual age for finishing high school and going on to college or getting a full-time job.

American parents may seem to be less strict than parents in some other cultures. But rules and discipline vary a lot from family to family; while some parents are lenient, others are strict.

**strict**—Severe; requiring complete obedience

**discipline**—Training to produce obedience and self-control

**lenient**—Mild, not severe

# Cultural Exchange

*A. Tell whether these sentences about the United States are true or false.*

1. American parents seem to be more strict than parents in other cultures.

2. It is acceptable for children over eighteen to move out.

3. Most students finish high school when they are twenty.

4. Parents encourage the children to make their own decisions.

5. Parents encourage children to get jobs outside the home.

*B. Answer these questions about your culture in writing or aloud.*

**In a typical family . . .**

1. What household chores do children have?

2. Are children expected to be "seen but not heard"?

3. What are acceptable forms of punishment?

4. How do children express respect for parents? (words? obedience? hugs and kisses?)

5. Do unmarried sons move out? If so, at what age? Can unmarried daughters move out? At what age?

---

**C.** *Discuss these questions with your classmates.*

1. In American culture, most children are encouraged to be independent. Do you think that is a good idea? Why or why not?

2. In American culture, many parents give children a weekly allowance or spending money. Do you think that is a good idea? Why or why not? Explain.

3. In your culture, are working children expected to give money to the family? Explain.

4. In your culture, are family matters discussed openly in front of the children?

5. In your culture, if children have problems who do they discuss them with?

6. Do you think that children in American culture seem less respectful to their parents than in your culture? Explain.

7. Are there any American ways of raising children that you would like to follow? Describe. Are there any American ways of raising children that you would never follow? Describe.

# Expansion

*In groups of at least four people, choose one of the parent/child issues listed below. Each group divides into two sides—one agreeing with the child, the other agreeing with the parents. Each side makes a list of reasons why their position on the issue is correct. Then both sides present their reasons to the rest of the class. The other class members can vote to see whether they support the child or the parents.*

1. A son wants to quit college for a high-paying job. His parents want him to complete his education.

2. A daughter wants to get married. The parents do not approve of the man she wants to marry because he has no job.

3. A daughter wants to become an airline pilot. Her parents feel this is not the proper job for a woman.

4. The eldest son has been offered an excellent job out of the country. His parents do not want him to leave.

5. A child has musical ability but is only interested in rock and roll. Her parents object to this music.

# Follow-Up

A. *Give a brief oral or written report. Choose number 1 or 2.*

1. Tell about a time when you did something against your parents' rules.

2. Tell about a time when your child did something against your rules.

*In your report, consider including some of the following details:*

How long ago did this happen?

Where were you living at the time?

How old was the child?

What rule was broken?

What happened afterward?

How did the child feel?

How did the parent feel?

Was there any kind of punishment? Describe.

What did you learn from this experience?

B. *Pretend you are a parent. Your eighteen-year-old has asked your permission to move out of the house into an inexpensive apartment. Your child wants to do this because he or she wants to learn how to become more independent, learn how to handle money, and make his or her own decisions.*

*Write a letter to your child; try to convince him or her why you think it is a good or bad idea for the child to move out. Give some reasons why you think the way you do.*

# U n i t 16
# *The Classroom*

## ? Do you know…

1. Do American teachers generally prefer students to be quiet or to ask questions?

2. How do teachers react when students disagree with them?

# School Daze

*Read the story.*

Call me Henry. I grew up in Vietnam, where we usually don't ask questions or have much contact with teachers. Rarely will students raise their hands. From the day I entered kindergarten and all the way through high school, I just listened and took notes in class. Each evening it was my responsibility to memorize the materials that were presented in class that day. There were no discussions, debates, or challenges to the teachers' point of view. The teachers were always right because they were the teachers. They knew the stuff better than me.

When I came to the United States the school system surprised me. My classes were hardly ever quiet. One day we had a discussion on the topic of gun control. Everyone participated in it. The class atmosphere was exciting and fun. The arguing went on until the end of the class, and everyone seemed to enjoy it. To my surprise the teacher encouraged the discussion and listened to what the students had to say. This felt very different to me. The teacher was treating the students like friends, not like in Vietnam where teachers kept their distance from the students. Hearing the discussion, I learned there were many different opinions on the question of gun control. I also learned that a person who is good at communicating can persuade other people to change their points of view.

Thinking back on school days in Vietnam, I realized that I wasn't very good at communicating with people because I hadn't had the practice. I couldn't even express myself clearly about the materials that I learned in Vietnam. Fortunately, during the gun-control discussion, the teacher didn't call on me to state my opinion.

From that day I have been working on expressing my thoughts in a clear manner so that people can understand what I mean.

**daze**—To be in a state of confusion

**School Daze**—A play on words; the usual expression is "School Days," meaning the time spent in school; by changing *days* to *daze*, it means the confusion caused by being in school

# Comprehension

**A.** *Tell whether these sentences are true or false.*

1. In Vietnam, Henry only listened, took notes, and memorized.
2. In Vietnam, the teacher was always right.
3. Henry was bored in his American classroom.
4. Henry was very surprised by his American classroom.
5. The American teacher was very strict and the students were afraid of him.
6. Henry learned there were different sides to the issue of gun control.
7. Henry learned about the importance of good communication skills.

**B.** *Answer these questions.*

1. What are Vietnamese students supposed to do in class?
2. What surprised Henry about his American classroom?
3. How did the American students respond to the topic of gun control?
4. How did the teacher respond to the noise and differences of opinion?
5. What is Henry trying to do to improve his American classroom abilities?

**C.** *Give your opinion.*

1. What do you think is a more effective way to learn: memorization or discussion? Explain.
2. Do you think Henry will find it easy or hard to adapt to the American system? Explain.
3. Do you think it is easier or harder to be a teacher in Vietnam (according to what Henry described) or the United States?
4. Do you approve of the way Henry's teacher dealt with the issue of gun control?

**D.** *Now add your own ideas to the story.*

1. Which does Henry like better, the Vietnamese or the American educational system?
2. Since Henry was reluctant to participate in discussions, what did his classmates think about him?
3. What did the teacher think about Henry's lack of participation?

**E.** *Compare yourself with Henry.*

1. What did Henry learn?
2. What did you learn from Henry's story?

# Vocabulary ▐▐▐▶

*What is the meaning of the underlined word or phrase? Circle the letter of the correct answer.*

1. The class atmosphere was <u>exciting</u>.
   a. The air in the room was warm.
   b. The class was stimulating.

2. It was my <u>responsibility</u> to memorize the materials.
   a. I had to memorize the materials.
   b. My parents had to help me learn my lessons.

3. We don't have much <u>contact</u> with the teacher.
   a. We don't have a written agreement with the teacher.
   b. We don't get to know our teachers very well.

4. We had a discussion about <u>gun control</u>.
   a. We had a discussion about laws to reduce the use of guns.
   b. We had a discussion about how to use guns.

5. There were no <u>debates</u>.
   a. They could have differences of opinion.
   b. They could not have differences of opinion.

6. There were no <u>challenges</u> to the teacher's point of view.
   a. They could question the teacher's point of view.
   b. The couldn't question the teacher's point of view.

7. A person who is good at communicating can <u>persuade other people to change their points of view</u>.
   a. A person who is good at communicating can convince other people to change their minds.
   b. A person who is good at communicating can accept other people's point of view.

8. In Vietnam, teachers <u>kept their distance</u> from the students.
   a. In Vietnam, teachers did not get physically or emotionally close to students.
   b. In Vietnam, teachers disliked the students.

9. I <u>took notes</u> in class.
   a. I wrote messages to my classmates.
   b. I wrote down what the teacher said.

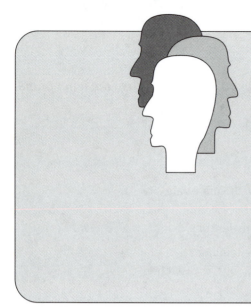

# CULTURE CAPSULE

Teachers will not be angry if students disagree. Actually, they like students who speak up in class by asking questions and giving their own ideas. Because it encourages participation, teachers often use small-group discussion to ask for student opinions. Generally, teachers do not require memorization of many facts.

Students are also encouraged to participate in after-school activities such as sports teams, orchestra, and leadership classes. It is generally believed that students who have interests beyond getting good grades will have more chance of getting into better colleges and universities.

# Cultural  Exchange

**A.** *Tell whether these sentences about the United States are true or false.*

1. Teachers get angry if students disagree.

2. Teachers like students who speak up in class.

3. Teachers require a lot of memorization of facts.

4. Students are encouraged to participate in after-school activities.

5. If students participate in extra activities, they will have more chance of getting into better colleges and universities.

*B. Fill in the chart, and then share your answers with your classmates.*

| Concerning School in Your Country ... | |
|---|---|
| At what age does a child start school? | |
| How many years are required? | |
| Is it free? If not, how much does it cost? | |
| Is physical punishment allowed? | |
| Do students wear uniforms? | |
| How much homework is given? | |
| Is questioning of teachers encouraged? | |
| Do students raise their hands when they want the teacher to call on them? | |
| Do students stand when the teacher enters the room? | |

*C. Discuss these questions with your classmates.*

1. In your culture, is it all right for a student to copy someone else's work or copy from the book? Explain.

2. In your culture, how is it determined who goes to college?

3. In your culture, do teachers treat students in an informal way, or is there a distance between them? Explain.

4. In your culture, is it customary to give gifts to teachers? If so, on what occasions?

5. In your culture, is it acceptable for a student to question the grade a teacher gives? Explain.

6. In your culture, what kind of academic preparation must a teacher have?

7. In your culture, is teaching a highly respected profession? Is teaching a well-paid profession?

8. From what you have learned or seen in movies or on TV, do you think teachers give more or less homework in the United States than in your country? Is this good or bad? Why?

9. Do you think you would like to attend a school in the United States? Why or why not?

# Expansion

*Work in pairs. One person is an elementary school teacher, Mr. Roberts. The other is a parent of any one of the students listed below. The parent phones Mr. Roberts and asks him to give a progress report on the child. Begin as in the example below. Use the information provided and your imagination to continue the conversation.*

MRS. BAKER:  *Hello, Mr. Roberts? This is Mrs. Baker, Lino's mother. Can you please tell me how my son is doing?*

MR. ROBERTS:  *Mrs. Baker, Lino is doing very well in math, but . . . .*

| Name of Student | Behavior | Reading | Math | Social Studies |
|---|---|---|---|---|
| Melissa Costa | talks too much | B | B+ | A |
| Lino Baker | troublemaker | D | A | C |
| Corie Espinoza | perfect | A | A | A |
| Tony Cobb | seems disinterested | D | D | F |
| Jasmine Choy | obedient | C− | D | C− |
| Eric Miller | often absent or late | C | C | C |

# Follow-Up

**A.** *Give a brief oral or written report. Tell about the worst or best teacher you ever had. In your report, consider including some of the following details:*

What was your teacher's name?

What subject did this person teach?

At what school?

Where was the school located?

How long ago did you have this teacher?

What made this teacher so wonderful or so terrible? Give an example to show this.

How did this teacher affect your attitude toward school?

How did this teacher affect your attitude toward teachers?

*B. From the list of subjects commonly taught in secondary schools in the United States, choose the six subjects that you would most like to study. If you are not sure what these subjects are, look them up in the dictionary. Compare your choices with your classmates' choices.*

| | | |
|---|---|---|
| algebra | art | biology |
| calculus | chemistry | drama |
| driver education | English | French |
| German | geometry | health |
| history | journalism | music |
| physical education | physics | psychology |
| Spanish | trigonometry | word processing |

**Your Choices**

1. _____

2. _____

3. _____

4. _____

5. _____

6. _____

# UNIT 17

# *The Changing Role of Women*

## ? Do you know...

1. In what ways has the role of women been changing over the past twenty or thirty years?

2. When a man and a woman go out on a date, who usually pays?

# Who Pays the Check?

*Read the story.*

I am Jennifer. In my senior year in high school, there were many exciting activities like dances, homecoming picnics, sports contests against the teachers, and, of course, the prom!

Prom night was coming, and tickets went on sale. They cost $89 for a couple. Single guys roamed the school, looking for girls to ask out. A friend told me that one of his friends wanted to go to the prom with me. Eventually I met the friend, Eddie, and we got along just fine. Gentleman-like, Eddie offered to pay for our prom tickets. However, he insisted that I pay for the prom pictures, and trying to do my part, I agreed. At the prom, everything went just great. We danced, ate, and chatted for at least five hours.

After the prom, we went to a restaurant and had dinner. The dinner was great, too, but when it was over, the trouble began. Eddie just sat there, even though he had finished eating. Thinking that he was tired, I just sat there too. Then it turned out that Eddie expected me to pay for the meal. I was horrified because, according to Chinese customs, a guy always pays for everything when he asks a girl out. I was already surprised when Eddie had insisted that I pay for the prom pictures, but this was too much for me. Eventually I paid and Eddie drove me home. I did not talk to him for a very long time. Later on, I found out that there is an American custom of "splitting the bill," where each individual pays half. It took me a long time to adapt to this custom!

**homecoming**—A school celebration welcoming back former students

**picnic**—A party where food is eaten outdoors

**prom**—A formal school dance for students who are about to graduate

**roamed**—Wandered

**chatted**—Talked in a friendly, informal manner

**adapt**—Change to fit into a new situation

# Comprehension

**A.** *Tell whether these sentences are true or false.*

1. Prom tickets cost $89 for a couple.

2. Jennifer and Eddie were friends from class.

3. Eddie wanted Jennifer to pay for the prom tickets.

4. Eddie wanted Jennifer to pay for the dinner.

5. Jennifer had a great time at the prom.

6. Sharing costs on a date is both a Chinese custom and an American custom.

7. Jennifer is now used to the custom of splitting the bill with a boy.

**B.** *Answer these questions.*

1. What were some of the senior-year activities at Jennifer's high school?

2. How did Jennifer meet Eddie?

3. What was the first thing that surprised Jennifer?

4. Why did Eddie just sit when the meal was over?

5. Why was Jennifer surprised that she had to pay for the food?

6. How did Jennifer treat Eddie after that night?

**C.** *Give your opinion.*

1. Do you think it was fair for Eddie to want Jennifer to pay for the pictures? Why or why not?

2. How could the situation at the restaurant have been avoided?

3. Do you think Jennifer should have been so angry with Eddie? Explain.

4. Do you like the American custom of splitting expenses on dates? Explain your answer.

5. Do you think it is reasonable to expect high school students to spend so much money for prom activities?

**D.** *Now add your own ideas to the story.*

1. How does Jennifer feel when she realizes Eddie wants her to pay the check? (confused? surprised? angry? other?)

2. How does Eddie feel when Jennifer is displeased about paying the check? (confused? surprised? angry? other?)

3. Does Eddie understand there was a problem of cultural differences?

4. Will Eddie ever ask Jennifer out on a date again?

5. Does Jennifer remain angry with Eddie? Will she only want to date Chinese boys in the future?

**E.** *Compare yourself with Jennifer.*

1. What did Jennifer learn?

2. What did you learn from Jennifer's story?

# Vocabulary

*What is the meaning of the underlined word? Circle the letter of the correct answer.*

1. Single guys roamed the school.
   a. gang members
   b. boys without steady girlfriends

2. I found out about splitting the bill.
   a. Each person pays half of the check.
   b. One person cuts the check in half with a knife or scissors.

3. Eddie insisted that I pay for the prom pictures.
   a. agreed
   b. demanded

4. It took Jennifer a long time to adapt to the custom.
   a. appeal
   b. adjust

5. Eddie offered to pay for the prom tickets.
   a. volunteered
   b. refused

6. We danced and chatted.
   a. argued
   b. had a friendly conversation

## CULTURE CAPSULE

Women's roles have been changing. Thirty years ago most married women were housewives and did not work outside the home. Today, most women have jobs, including jobs—such as truck driver or business executive—that used to be held only by men.

With the changes in roles have come changes in customs. Women used to expect that men would open doors for them, but now they open their own. When a man invited a woman out for dinner, he was expected to pay for everything. Today, a woman might share the expenses when she goes out with a man. She can be the one who calls him up and asks him out. She might even pay the expenses for the entire date.

# Cultural Exchange

**A.** *Tell whether these sentences about the United States are true or false.*

1. Today most married women are housewives and do not work outside the home.

2. Women cannot be truck drivers or business executives.

3. Women used to expect that men would open doors for them.

4. Women still expect men to open doors for them.

5. Sometimes a woman will invite a man out on a date and pay for all the expenses.

**B.** *Fill in the chart, and then share your answers with your classmates.*

| Concerning Males and Females in Your Country . . . | |
|---|---|
| Do sons and daughters have the same household chores? | |
| Do sons and daughters receive the same amount of education? | |
| Are sons and daughters equally valued? | |
| After marriage, are daughters closer to their husband's family than their own family? | |
| Can women invite men out on dates? | |
| Can women pay when going out with men? | |
| Is it acceptable for women not to marry? | |
| Do married women with children work outside the home? | |
| In a divorce, who generally gets custody of the children? | |

*C. Discuss these questions with your classmates.*

1. Are single mothers (those divorced or never married) approved or disapproved of in your culture? From what you have learned or seen in movies or on TV, are they approved or disapproved of in American culture?

2. In your culture, are husbands looked down upon if their wives work outside the home? How do you think this compares with American culture?

3. In your culture, is it acceptable for a woman to be out alone at night? How do you think this compares with American culture?

4. What are the usual kinds of jobs that women have in your country? Would men ever have these jobs?

5. Are there any jobs held by women in the United States that would not be allowed for women in your country? Are there any jobs held by women in your country that you don't think American women would have?

6. Do you think that the changing role of women has had a positive or a negative effect on American culture? Explain.

7. If you are a woman, what part of the American woman's role would you like to try? What part would you not like to try? If you are a man, what part of the American woman's role would you like or dislike for your wife or daughter?

# Expansion

*Divide into groups of six to eight people. Each group chooses one of the issues listed below. Half of each group should make a list of reasons why they agree with the statement, and the other half should make a list of reasons why they disagree with the statement. Have both sides present their reasons to the rest of the class. The class can vote to see whether they agree or disagree. You can add other issues if you like.*

1. It is time to elect a woman president of the United States.

2. Women should be able to become fighter pilots.

3. Girls should be allowed to play high school football.

4. Husbands should equally share housework and child-care responsibilities with their wives.

5. Married women should stay home and take care of their children.

6. If boys want to play with dolls they should be allowed to do so.

7. Single women should invite men out on dates.

8. Single women should share dating expenses with men.

# Follow-Up ✓

**A.** *Give a brief oral or written report. Choose number 1 or 2.*

1. How would your life be different if you had been born the opposite sex?

2. When you were growing up, did your parents treat sons and daughters differently? If so, how?

*If you choose number 1, consider including some of the following details:*

How would your parents have treated you differently?

How would your education be different? Give an example.

How would your work be different?

How would your financial situation be different?

Would you have more influence or power? Less influence or power?

How would your romantic life be different?

How would your friendships be different?

Would your life be a happier one if you had been born the opposite sex? Explain.

*If you choose number 2, consider including some of the following details:*

How were the household chores the same or different?

How were the educational expectations the same or different?

Could sons and daughters stay out until the same hour?

Could daughters go out alone? Could sons?

When you have your own sons and daughters, will you treat them the same way your parents did? Why or why not?

Now that you have your own sons and daughters, have you raised them the same way your parents did? Why or why not?

**B.** *Make two lists. For one list write down all the advantages in being female. For the other list write down all the advantages in being male. Which list is longer? What does this tell you? Compare your lists with those of your classmates.*

# Attitudes Toward Aging

## ? Do you know...

1. Do many Americans look forward to growing older? Why or why not?

2. What are some disadvantages of growing older?

# Jack's Tale

*Read the story.*

When my family emigrated from a small village in Canton, China, we brought not only our luggage, but also our village's rules, customs, and superstitions. One of the rules is that youngsters should always respect elders. Unfortunately, this rule resulted in my very first embarrassment in the United States.

I had a part-time job as a waiter in a Chinese restaurant. One time, when I was serving food to a middle-aged couple, the wife asked me how the food could be served so quickly. I told her that I had made sure they got their food quickly because I always respect the elderly. As soon as I said that, her face showed great displeasure. My manager, who had overheard, took me aside and gave me a long lecture about how sensitive Americans are and how they dislike the description "old." I then walked back to the table and apologized to the wife. After the couple listened to my explanation, they understood that the incident was caused by cultural differences, so they laughed and were no longer angry.

In my village in China, people are proud of being older. Not that many people survive to the age of fifty or sixty, and people who reach such an age have the most knowledge and experience. Youngsters always respect older people because they know they can learn from this valuable experience.

However, in the United States aging is considered a problem since "old" means that a person is going to retire or that the body is not functioning so well. Here many people try to avoid old age by doing exercises or jogging, and women put on makeup hoping to look young. When I told the couple in the restaurant that I respect the elderly, they got angry because this made them feel they had failed to retain their youth. I had told them something they didn't want to hear.

As a result of this experience, I have changed the way I am with older people. This does not mean that I don't respect them anymore; I still respect them, but now I don't express my feelings through words.

**superstitions**—Beliefs that are not based on reason but are based on magic or old ideas

# Comprehension

**A.** *Tell whether these sentences are true or false.*

1. When Jack came to America he only brought his luggage.

2. Jack brought the couple their food very fast because he wanted a good tip.

3. When Jack called the couple "elderly," they were displeased.

4. Jack's manager wanted to fire him.

5. After Jack apologized, the couple left the restaurant angry.

6. Jack respects older people because they have the most knowledge and experience.

7. Jack no longer respects the elderly.

**B.** *Answer these questions.*

1. What is one of the rules that Jack brought with him from China?

2. What did Jack do that offended the couple?

3. What did Jack's manager explain to Jack?

4. How did the couple respond after Jack apologized?

5. According to Jack, why was the couple upset?

6. As a result of this experience how has Jack changed?

**C.** *Give your opinion.*

1. Do you think Jack's boss handled the situation well? Explain.

2. Do you think Jack handled the situation well after he apologized? Explain.

3. Do you think the couple handled the situation well after Jack apologized? Explain. What other reaction might they have had?

4. Do you think Jack made the right decision not to express his feelings through words anymore? Why or why not?

5. What is your opinion of Jack?

**D.** *Now add your own ideas to the story.*

1. Is the lady angry, hurt, or shocked by what Jack tells her?

2. How does the manager feel? Is he angry? Is he worried about losing these customers? Is he sympathetic toward the customers? Is he understanding of Jack's ignorance of American ways? Explain.

3. Does Jack feel guilty or embarrassed when the manager talks to him? Does he worry about losing his job?

*Continued on the following page*

4. What does Jack say to the lady?

5. In the end, is the lady sympathetic toward Jack? Or is she still a little angry?

**E.** *Compare yourself with Jack.*

1. What did Jack learn?

2. What did you learn from Jack's story?

# Vocabulary ▐▐▐▶

*What is the meaning of the underlined word? Circle the letter of the correct answer.*

1. My family <u>emigrated</u> from a small village in China.
   a. left
   b. originated

2. They felt they had failed to <u>retain</u> their youth.
   a. keep
   b. return

3. We brought our <u>luggage</u>.
   a. clothing
   b. suitcases

4. I <u>apologized</u> to the wife.
   a. said I was sorry
   b. applauded

5. My manager <u>overheard</u> me.
   a. stood over me
   b. listened to what I had said

6. In China, people are <u>proud</u> of being older.
   a. self-respecting
   b. self-reliant

7. My manager took me <u>aside</u>.
   a. outside
   b. in private

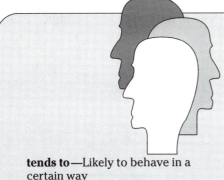

# CULTURE CAPSULE

America tends to be a youth-oriented culture. Although some cultures value getting old, in America people tend to value being young. This is shown, for example, by the large amounts of money spent on products that prevent wrinkles or cover up gray hair. Being a "senior citizen" (sixty-five years of age or older) brings certain privileges, such as reduced prices for theater and travel tickets. But because of society's attitudes, many people probably do not look forward to growing old. However, attitudes toward aging might be changing. In a sense, the American population is aging; by the year 2030, over 20 percent of Americans will be sixty-five years or older. As the population ages, Americans are becoming more aware that older people have a lot to contribute to society.

**tends to**—Likely to behave in a certain way

**youth-oriented**—Believing in being and staying young

**wrinkles**—Creases and lines on the skin, especially the face

**privileges**—Special rights or advantages given to an individual or group

# Cultural Exchange

**A.** *Tell whether these sentences about the United States are true or false.*

1. Americans value being young.

2. They spend lots of money on covering up wrinkles and gray hair.

3. They give no benefits to senior citizens.

4. Most people look forward to growing old.

5. By the year 2030 over 40 percent of Americans will be sixty-five years or older.

*B. Fill in the chart, and then share your answers with your classmates.*

| When It Comes to Aging in Your Country . . . | |
|---|---|
| Is it acceptable to ask people their age? | |
| At what age do people retire? | |
| At what age are people considered old? | |
| Do people try to slow the effects of aging? If so, how? (hair dye? surgery? other?) | |
| What are the privileges of aging? (discounted prices? respect? other?) | |

*C. Discuss these questions with your classmates.*

1. In your culture, do you celebrate birthdays? Which birthdays are the special ones?

2. In your culture, where do the elderly live, and with whom?

3. In your culture, does one particular child take care of elderly parents, or do all the children share the responsibility? Explain.

4. In your culture, are elderly men treated the same as elderly women? Explain.

5. How are the attitudes toward the elderly and aging in America the same as or different from those in your country?

6. What do you see as disadvantages of getting old in the United States compared to your country? Do you see any advantages?

# Expansion

*Conduct a survey on attitudes about aging. With a partner, ask and answer the following questions. Then compare answers with your classmates. You may also want to ask people outside of the classroom for their opinions.*

1. Do you think there is a certain age at which you will be old? If so, about what age?

2. When you are old would you consider:

   a. lying about your age?

   b. changing your gray hair to another color?

   c. using cosmetics to make you seem younger?

   d. having surgery to make your face look younger?

   e. wearing clothes made for younger people?

3. What kinds of things do you look forward to doing when you get old?

4. Do you consider older people more valuable than younger people, younger people more valuable than older people, or both equally valuable? Explain.

# Follow-Up

*A. Give a brief oral or written report. Tell about an older person in your life who has influenced you. In your report, consider including some of the following details:*

Who is (was) the person?

What is (was) your relationship to this person?

Where does (did) this person live?

What does (did) this person look like?

How did you meet this person?

What makes this person so special? Give an example.

How has this person affected your life?

**B.** *Television report. Watch thirty to sixty minutes of TV and take notes about the older people you see in the commercials and in the shows. How are older people depicted? Some possible descriptions are given below. Add any others you can think of.*

**Are They . . . ?**

| | | |
|---|---|---|
| helpful | important | wise |
| leaders | insignificant | weak |
| stupid | grouchy | sweet |

stars, or minor characters

problems, or problem solvers

*Bring your report to class and compare it with your classmates' reports. After hearing all the reports, is there anything you can conclude about how older people are depicted?*

# UNIT 19

# Stereotypes and Prejudice

? Do you know...

1. What is prejudice? Is prejudice common in the
   United States?

2. What can be done to fight prejudice?

# Sticks and Stones

*Read the story.*

My name is Teresa. My parents are from Mexico but moved to the United States, where I was born. When I was twelve years old I was bused from my neighborhood to a community nearby for junior high school. My reaction when I got to the school was one of culture shock. The majority of students, teachers, and staff were Anglo. I had never been in such an environment before. Up to then I had been in a completely Hispanic neighborhood and school. The first thing that ran through my head was, where have I been?

I felt as if I was in another world of people who looked different, acted differently, spoke and dressed differently. I didn't know how to behave or what to say. They wore what I later discovered to be designer jeans and backpacks. They also seemed to be wealthy, because they paid cash for their meals while I used reduced meal tickets.

I didn't have any friends at first. I didn't know any of the students who rode the bus with me, and in most of my classes I was the only Hispanic. I was shy and embarrassed. I felt very intimidated by all these very verbal and confident individuals. I also felt vibrations of hate and resentment from these people, although I wasn't sure why. I had no one to talk to or turn to for help who I thought would be able to understand. I had no Hispanic role models.

During the first week of school, there was an incident. As my bus was leaving the school, a bunch of Anglo kids began throwing eggs at the bus and screaming, "Go home, beaners!" I had no idea what a "beaner" was or why the kids would be so cruel. This incident stayed with me. I earned A's in most of my classes. As time went on, I became friends with other Hispanics and with Anglo kids. But I still felt hurt, mad, and a little confused. Deep inside I knew that the majority of the Anglo kids did not want any "beaners" in their school. They must have felt invaded, and I

**sticks and stones**—The first words of a verse that parents teach children to say to other children who call them bad names: *Sticks and stones may break my bones, but names can never hurt me.*

**(to be) bused**—Sending children by bus from their own school to a generally better school

**intimidated**—Frightened, often caused by threats of violence

**vibrations**—Emotional sensations

**role models**—People to look up to, copying their achievements and behavior

**cruel**—Feeling pleasure in the pain or suffering of another person

**invaded**—Taken under control by outsiders

think that since they did not really know many Hispanics, they probably had hundreds of stereotypes about us.

How did I feel at the end of my first year? I felt that my experience had been very meaningful and educational. I was amazed by how much I had learned about another part of society. My attitudes toward these "other" people had changed greatly. Above all, I felt that my eyes had been opened to more of what life had to offer and that I had learned quite a lot academically, probably more than I would have learned if I had gone to junior high school in my neighborhood.

**stereotypes**—Fixed patterns that represent a type of person or event, usually negative

# Comprehension

**A.** *Tell whether these sentences are true or false.*

1. Before junior high school, Teresa had never been in a school with Anglos.

2. Teresa's first reaction to her new school was culture shock.

3. Teresa made friends at the new school right away.

4. Teresa paid cash for her meals.

5. Some Anglo students called the Hispanic students "beaners."

6. Some Anglo students threw eggs at Teresa's bus.

7. Teresa did not get good grades at her new school.

8. At the end of the year, Teresa decided she would switch back to the junior high school in her neighborhood.

**B.** *Answer these questions.*

1. Why was Teresa shocked by her new school?

2. How did the students dress there?

3. What incident occurred during Teresa's first week of school?

4. Why does Teresa think the students acted that way?

5. Besides academic opportunities, what else did Teresa get out of being bused?

**C.** *Give your opinion.*

1. Why do you think the students threw eggs at the bus and called the Hispanic students names?

2. Do you agree with Teresa that even though she eventually became friends with the Anglo kids, deep inside they did not want Hispanics at their school? Why or why not?

*Continued on the following page*

3. Do you agree with Teresa that it is valuable to step outside one's own territory and see what other opportunities there are? Why or why not?

4. Do you think busing is a good way to achieve this?

**D.** *Now add your own ideas to the story.*

1. How does Teresa feel after the other students yell names and throw eggs at the bus?

2. Are the classmates mean or ignorant? Do they feel guilty?

3. What do the teachers do about the situation?

4. What does the bus driver do about the situation?

5. What happens to the students who threw eggs and called names? Are they disciplined? How?

**E.** *Compare yourself with Teresa.*

1. What did Teresa learn?

2. What did you learn from Teresa's story?

# Vocabulary ||||➡

*Replace the underlined word(s) in the sentences with the words below.*

| | | | |
|---|---|---|---|
| environment | resentment | amazed | confident |
| academically | reaction | backpacks | designer jeans |

1. For Teresa it was a new place.

2. She felt displeasure from these people.

3. Scholastically, she learned a lot from her new school.

4. They wore expensive pants and book carriers.

5. Teresa's response to her new school was culture shock.

6. The other students were so unafraid.

7. At the end of the first year Teresa was astonished by how much she had learned.

# CULTURE CAPSULE

The United States has often been called a "melting pot"—a place where people from many different countries blend together and all become Americans. But many people argue that this description is not accurate. They say the United States is more like a salad bowl—many ingredients are tossed together but never completely blend. On the one hand, this is what makes the United States more interesting: People are not just Americans; they are Americans and something else. On the other hand, the differences have sometimes led to problems—to stereotypes and prejudice, to discrimination, and at times even to violence.

With the civil rights movement, led by African Americans in the 1950s and 1960s, some important changes were made to fight prejudice and discrimination. Busing, sending African American and Hispanic children from poor school districts to Anglo schools in better neighborhoods, was an attempt to provide equal educational opportunities. As American society becomes more racially and ethnically mixed, many more changes must be made.

**blend**—To mix together into a smooth and unified substance

**tossed**—Mixed lightly

**prejudice**—Unfair and often unfavorable feeling or opinion not based on reason or enough knowledge

**discrimination**—Unfair treatment

**civil rights movement**—Organized actions to obtain equal rights, privileges, and protection for minorities

# Cultural Exchange

*A. Tell whether these sentences about the United States are true or false.*

1. Some people call the country a melting pot.

2. Some people call the country a salad bowl.

3. There is no discrimination or prejudice.

4. Busing is an attempt to give children in poorer neighborhoods a chance for a better education.

5. Native Americans led the civil rights movement in the 1950s and 1960s.

***B.*** *Discuss these questions with your classmates.*

1. In your country, are there any ethnic, racial, or religious groups that faced prejudice and discrimination in the past? Do any continue to face prejudice and discrimination today? Explain.

2. Are there any other groups in your country that you think face some prejudice and discrimination? For example, are physically disabled people discriminated against? People who are divorced? Single mothers? Explain.

3. In your country, are there any kinds of government policies or laws to discourage discrimination?

4. In your country, do people of different ethnic groups usually socialize with one another? Explain.

5. In your country, do people object to marriages between persons of different ethnic groups, races, or religions? Explain.

6. In your country, do people from different groups live in separate neighborhoods?

7. Do you think you would feel discriminated against in the United States? Why?

8. Have you ever seen or known anyone in your country who was prejudiced against Americans? Explain.

# Expansion

*Work in groups. Choose one of the two situations below. In each of the situations someone faces a problem. In your group, discuss the three possible solutions listed and the consequences of the solutions. Choose one of the solutions and compare your group's decision with those of other groups.*

1. Mike is a very successful sales representative and an outstanding employee. He has recently begun playing with a rock band after work and has let his hair grow to shoulder length. Mike's company wants him to cut his hair. They say it is bad for the company image for him to look that way. Mike says that as long as he is doing his job well, which he is, the company has no right to tell him how to wear his hair. But the company threatens to fire him unless he cuts it.

   Mike says that the company is discriminating against him. What do you think?

   Our group has decided that:

   a. Mike should quit and find another company that will accept his hair length.

   b. Mike should cut his hair and stay with the company.

   c. Mike should take legal action against his company so that he can keep his hair as long as he wants and still continue working there.

2. A corporation has asked its office manager, Leila, to move and set up a new department of the company in a city some 2,000 miles away. In exchange, the company promises to promote Leila to a higher position. Leila moves her family, successfully opens up the department, has it running smoothly, and the company praises Leila for her accomplishment. However, when the time comes for Leila's promotion, the company backs down and puts a male employee into the higher position instead.

Leila claims that the company is discriminating against her because she is a woman. What do you think?

Our group has decided that:

a. Leila should quit and find another job.

b. Leila should accept the company's decision.

c. Leila should take legal action against the company.

# Follow-Up

**A.** *Give a brief oral or written report. Choose number 1 or 2.*

1. Tell about a time when you were the victim of prejudice because of religion, culture, race, sex, age, or physical disability.

2. Tell about a time when you felt prejudiced against someone else because of that person's religion, culture, race, sex, age, or physical disability.

*In your report, consider including some of the following details:*

How long ago did this happen?

Where were you living at the time?

Who were the persons involved?

What happened?

How did you react?

How did others react?

What was the immediate effect of this experience?

What have you learned from this experience?

**B.** *With a partner, use an encyclopedia to research Native Americans, a group that has suffered a lot from prejudice and discrimination in the United States, so much so that today most live in isolated, poor conditions on land called "reservations."*

1. Choose a Native American tribe from the list below, or choose another tribe, and write down information about it.

2. Tell where the tribe is located, give some information about its culture (e.g., clothing, housing, language, customs, arts and crafts), and if you can, find out how the tribe has changed over the years as a result of contact with other Americans.

3. Share the information with your classmates.

| | | |
|---|---|---|
| Apache | Klamath | Seminole |
| Arapaho | Mohican | Shoshone |
| Blackfoot | Navaho | Sioux |
| Chickasaw | Nez Percé | Tlingit |
| Iroquois | Pawnee | Winnebago |
| Kiowa | Pueblo | |

# UNIT 20

# *Religious Practices and Beliefs*

**?** Do you know...

1. What are some of the religions that are practiced in the United States?

2. Have you discovered any religious practices that have surprised you?

# The Surprise

*Read the story.*

I came from Mexico, and my name is Amalia. Like most people, my family came to the United States for better opportunities in employment and education. Learning a new language wasn't easy, and what was even more difficult was learning to live with people from different cultures—not just the American culture, but many other cultures, too. One of the embarrassing experiences I have had involved my best friend Silvia, who is from Venezuela and is a Jehovah's Witness.

When Silvia told me she was a Jehovah's Witness, I didn't know what that meant. She explained it was a religion. On her sixteenth birthday, Silvia invited me to her house. I was really excited. I thought there would be a party, so the day before I bought Silvia a present. It was an antique music box. When my dad dropped me off at her house I was surprised because the house seemed lonely and silent. I knocked at the door, and her mom answered. She greeted me with a kiss on the cheek and a hug. Then she invited me in. As I entered the living room, I saw a group of people. I greeted them and sat down. A few seconds later, Silvia came downstairs. As she greeted me with a hug and a kiss, I took out the present and said, "Happy Birthday!"

All of a sudden the people in the room stopped talking and stared at Silvia and me. I looked at Silvia with a puzzled look. She was just looking down at the ground with a face as red as a tomato. After a few minutes of silence, she said, "I'm sorry, but I can't accept your present. It was really sweet of you." I froze. I was embarrassed, hurt, and humiliated. Tears rolled down my cheeks. I didn't know what to do. Here I was in the middle of the room with all those people looking at me and not saying anything. I wished they would at least laugh at me or something.

After a few minutes I came to reality and ran out of the room. I ran all the way to the driveway. Silvia came running after me. Then she explained that in her religion, they did not celebrate birthdays or holidays

**Jehovah's Witness**—A Christian sect founded in the 1870s in Pennsylvania whose principles include that religious belief is most important

**froze**—Was unable to move

of any kind, and that the people in her living room were members of her congregation. She couldn't accept the present. It would have gotten her in trouble because it was like breaking the law. As I turned to look at her, I saw there were tears in her eyes. "So, I have to keep the present?" I asked. Sadly, she nodded yes, but she gave me a hug and I felt a little better.

As a result of this experience, I've learned not to make assumptions. Not everybody has the same traditions as I do. Now when I hear of a new religion I ask for information and make sure I don't have another misunderstanding.

**congregation**—Those belonging to the same religious group

**assumptions**—Things taken for granted without proof

# Comprehension

**A.** *Tell whether these sentences are true or false.*

1. Amalia's family came to the United States for better job and education opportunities.

2. Silvia's family came from Mexico.

3. "Jehovah's Witness" refers to a kind of religion.

4. When Amalia got to Silvia's house she could tell the people there were having a party.

5. The other people in the house were members of Silvia's family.

6. Amalia cried when Silvia did not accept the present.

**B.** *Answer these questions.*

1. What kind of present did Amalia buy for Silvia?

2. What happened when Amalia said "Happy Birthday" and gave her friend the present?

3. Why didn't Silvia accept the present?

4. How did Silvia feel about not accepting the present?

5. What did Amalia learn from this experience?

**C.** *Give your opinion.*

1. Do you think Silvia's mother should have tried to help Amalia understand? Why or why not?

2. Do you think Amalia should have run out of the house like she did? Why or why not?

*Continued on the following page*

3. Do you think that Silvia should have warned her friend in advance about Jehovah's Witnesses not celebrating birthdays? Why or why not?

4. Do you think that Amalia and Silvia will remain friends?

**D.** *Now add your own ideas to the story.*

1. After Silvia rejects Amalia's gift, how does Amalia feel? Does she feel shocked? Hurt? Otherwise?

2. Is Silvia embarrassed because other people are there?

3. Does Silvia feel sympathy for Amalia?

4. What do those other people think about Silvia? Are they angry? Explain.

5. What will Amalia's parents say when she returns home with the gift and tells them what happened?

**E.** *Compare yourself with Amalia.*

1. What did Amalia learn?

2. What did you learn from Amalia's story?

# Vocabulary

*Replace the underlined word(s) in the sentences with the words below.*

| | | | |
|---|---|---|---|
| opportunities | employment | involved | antique |
| congregation | dropped her off | humiliated | froze |

1. Amalia's family came to the United States for better <u>chances</u> to find <u>jobs</u>.

2. Amalia bought Silvia a music box that was <u>very old</u>.

3. When Silvia refused to accept Amalia's gift, Amalia felt <u>ashamed</u>.

4. Amalia was so embarrassed and hurt she <u>couldn't move</u>.

5. Silvia explained that the people in her living room were members of her <u>church group</u>.

6. Amalia's father drove her to Silvia's house and <u>let her out of the car</u>.

7. Amalia's embarrassing experience <u>concerned</u> her friend Silvia, a member of the Jehovah's Witnesses.

# CULTURE CAPSULE

The United States has no official religion, as the U.S. Constitution says that church and state (religion and government) must be kept separate. This is not surprising since many early settlers (like many later immigrants) came to the United States for religious freedom. For this reason, it is also not so surprising that the United States has thousands of religions. Over 90 percent of Americans are Christians, but Christianity in the United States includes many different groups.

Religion plays an important part in the lives of many Americans. In addition to being places of worship, churches and temples are centers for education, social activities, and community events.

**places of worship**—Where one goes to pray or practice a religion

# Cultural Exchange

*A. Tell whether these sentences about the United States are true or false.*

1. Places of worship also serve as centers for education, social activities, and community events.

2. There is no official religion.

3. There are a few hundred different religions.

4. Most Americans are Muslim.

5. Many of the early settlers came to the country seeking religious freedom.

*B.* Fill in the chart, and then share your answers with your classmates.

| When It Comes to Religion in Your Country, Describe . . . | |
|---|---|
| Name of religion(s)? | |
| Symbols? (cross? Star of David? crescent moon? other?) | |
| Leader's title? (monk? priest? minister? mullah? other?) | |
| Where does the congregation gather? (church? mosque? temple? home? other?) | |
| Special fasting days? (name of celebration? date?) | |
| Special feast days? (name of celebration? date?) | |
| Ways to deal with sin or transgression? (confession? fasting? offerings? other?) | |
| Kinds of offerings? (flowers? money? food? incense? other?) | |
| Rituals for babies? (naming? other?) When done? | |
| Baptism? At what age? Takes place where? | |
| Rituals on reaching adulthood? At what age for boys? for girls? Name of ceremony? | |
| Rituals for dead? (burial? cremation?) When done? What happens? | |
| Memorial ceremonies on anniversaries of death? What happens? | |
| Special blessings for food? (wine? grapes? noodles? rice? bread?) | |

# Expansion

*See how many names of members of twenty different American religions you can find hidden in the Word Search Game. Words can go up and down, forward and backward, and they may overlap.*

```
M E N N O N I T E I D E N C R E K A U Q
A P V D E B K S U E F B H N U I L S N J
E I O T S A T I P H D K I A N C N E I O
W S G S H C T D C L M C G R L S I V T O
F C K I L E A O R H X N J E D F N E A L
H O B T J I Q H I N D U F H O J Y N R X
S P C P T C A T H O L I C T R E G T I O
I A O A B T M E O B A E B U D H I H A D
W L L B G N O M R P C V Q L Y O J D N O
E I G P R E S B Y T E R I A N V L A U H
J A C E E I L I S N Q H S I M A M Y Q T
P N Z N T M E H A P O O V R D H I A J R
F B P T G H M O R H C M E G P S H D F O
J I K E R E X E K I S G H Y I W B V G N
N A O C B R W H T M B Q E F I G E O A
O H D O P M H O A Q F D Y Z M T N N H I
M A R S K C C A X F P K C Z E N J T H S
R B S T J Q A M G H V J A D L E B I K S
O M V A K F I N I Z Z A B D K S O S A U
M T D L B R A C D B U D D H I S T T R R
```

| | | |
|---|---|---|
| Amish | Jehovah's Witness | Pentecostal |
| Bahai | Jewish | Presbyterian |
| Baptist | Lutheran | Quaker |
| Buddhist | Mennonite | Russian Orthodox |
| Catholic | Methodist | Seventh-day Adventist |
| Episcopalian | Mormon | Unitarian |
| Hindu | Moslem | |

# Follow-Up ✓

**A.** *Give a brief oral or written report. Step by step, describe a ceremony that you enjoy from your own religion or a ceremony you have seen and enjoyed from another religion. When you do this be sure to use such words as:*

*First* (First the bells rang . . .)

*Next* or *Second* (Next the parents brought in the baby . . .)

*After that* (After that they threw rice . . .)

*Finally* or *Last of all* (Finally they threw dirt on the grave . . .)

**B.** *On a piece of paper illustrate a religious ceremony you have seen and enjoyed. Compare your drawing with your classmates' drawings.*

# ANSWER KEY

## UNIT ONE
### Comprehension A:
1. F    2. T    3. F    4. T    5. F    6. T    7. F    8. T

### Vocabulary:
1. b    2. a    3. b    4. b    5. a    6. a    7. b    8. b    9. a    10. a

### Cultural Exchange:
1. F    2. F    3. F    4. F    5. F

### Expansion:

## UNIT TWO
### Comprehension A:
1. T    2. F    3. F    4. F    5. F    6. T    7. F    8. T

### Vocabulary:
1. a    2. b    3. a    4. a    5. a    6. a

### Cultural Exchange:
1. F    2. T    3. T    4. T    5. F

# UNIT THREE

## Comprehension A:
1. F    2. F    3. T    4. T    5. F    6. T    7. T    8. T

## Vocabulary:
1. child abuse    2. principal    3. fever    4. traditional values    5. objects    6. marks
7. punished    8. advised

## Cultural Exchange:
1. F    2. F    3. T    4. T    5. F

## Expansion:

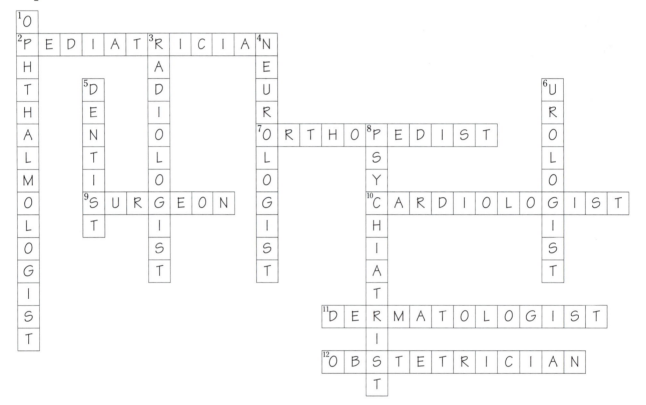

# UNIT FOUR

## Comprehension A:
1. F    2. T    3. F    4. T    5. F    6. F    7. F

## Vocabulary:
1. culture shock    2. chills    3. neighborhood    4. sacred    5. extracted    6. Hindu religion
7. ignorant    8. rewarding

## Cultural Exchange:
1. F    2. T    3. T    4. F    5. T

# UNIT FIVE
## Comprehension A:
1. T    2. T    3. F    4. F    5. T    6. F    7. T    8. T

## Vocabulary:
1. b    2. a    3. b    4. b    5. a    6. b    7. b

## Cultural Exchange:
1. F    2. F    3. T    4. T    5. F

# UNIT SIX
## Comprehension A:
1. T    2. F    3. T    4. F    5. T    6. T    7. F    8. F

## Vocabulary:
1. b    2. a    3. a    4. a    5. b    6. a

## Cultural Exchange:
1. F    2. F    3. T    4. F    5. F

# UNIT SEVEN
## Comprehension A:
1. F    2. T    3. T    4. T    5. F    6. F    7. T

## Vocabulary:
1. b    2. b    3. a    4. b    5. a    6. a    7. a

## Cultural Exchange:
1. T    2. F    3. F    4. T    5. T

# UNIT EIGHT
## Comprehension A:
1. F    2. F    3. T    4. F    5. T    6. F    7. T    8. F

## Vocabulary:
1. b    2. a    3. b    4. b    5. b    6. a    7. b

## Cultural Exchange:
1. T    2. F    3. F    4. T    5. T

# UNIT NINE

**Comprehension A:**
1. T    2. F    3. T    4. T    5. T    6. F    7. F    8. F

**Vocabulary:**
1. annoyed    2. interrupted    3. problems    4. local    5. avoid    6. observes    7. mistakes
8. address    9. proper    10. upset

**Cultural Exchange:**
1. T    2. F    3. T    4. F    5. T

# UNIT TEN

**Comprehension A:**
1. F    2. F    3. F    4. T    5. T    6. T    7. T

**Vocabulary:**
1. giggling    2. immediately    3. sunny    4. directly    5. adults    6. message    7. moist
8. grabbed    9. tightly    10. adapt

**Cultural Exchange:**
1. F    2. F    3. F    4. T    5. F

# UNIT ELEVEN

**Comprehension A:**
1. T    2. F    3. F    4. T    5. T    6. F    7. F

**Vocabulary:**
1. c    2. a    3. a    4. c    5. b    6. c    7. a

**Cultural Exchange:**
1. T    2. F    3. F    4. T    5. T

**Expansion (answers for American Culture):**
1. b    2. a or b    3. b    4. a    5. b    6. c

# UNIT TWELVE

**Comprehension A:**
1. T    2. F    3. F    4. F    5. F    6. F    7. F

**Vocabulary:**
1. a    2. a    3. b    4. b    5. a    6. b    7. a    8. a    9. a    10. a

**Cultural Exchange:**
1. F    2. T    3. F    4. F    5. T

# UNIT THIRTEEN
## Comprehension A:
1. F   2. F   3. T   4. F   5. T   6. F   7. T   8. F

## Vocabulary:
1. algebra   2. baggy   3. religion   4. appropriate   5. opinion   6. fabulous   7. cute
8. danger

## Cultural Exchange:
1. T   2. T   3. T   4. T   5. T

## Expansion:

# UNIT FOURTEEN
## Comprehension A:
1. T   2. T   3. F   4. T   5. F   6. T   7. T   8. F

## Vocabulary:
1. rude   2. customs, life-style   3. instantly   4. celebrations   5. eager   6. treated
7. expressions

## Cultural Exchange:
1. T   2. F   3. F   4. T   5. F

# UNIT FIFTEEN
## Comprehension A:
1. F   2. T   3. T   4. F   5. T   6. F   7. F   8. T

**Vocabulary:**
1. b   2. a   3. b   4. a   5. a   6. b   7. b   8. a   9. b

**Cultural Exchange:**
1. F   2. T   3. F   4. T   5. T

# UNIT SIXTEEN
**Comprehension A:**
1. T   2. T   3. F   4. T   5. F   6. T   7. T

**Vocabulary:**
1. b   2. a   3. b   4. a   5. b   6. b   7. a   8. a   9. b

**Cultural Exchange:**
1. F   2. T   3. F   4. T   5. T

# UNIT SEVENTEEN
**Comprehension A:**
1. T   2. F   3. F   4. T   5. T   6. F   7. T

**Vocabulary:**
1. b   2. a   3. b   4. b   5. a   6. b

**Cultural Exchange:**
1. F   2. F   3. T   4. F   5. T

# UNIT EIGHTEEN
**Comprehension A:**
1. F   2. F   3. T   4. F   5. F   6. T   7. F

**Vocabulary:**
1. a   2. a   3. b   4. a   5. b   6. a   7. b

**Cultural Exchange:**
1. T   2. T   3. F   4. F   5. F

# UNIT NINETEEN
**Comprehension A:**
1. T   2. T   3. F   4. F   5. T   6. T   7. F   8. F

**Vocabulary:**
1. environment   2. resentment   3. academically   4. designer jeans, backpacks   5. reaction
6. confident   7. amazed

**Cultural Exchange:**
1. T   2. T   3. F   4. T   5. F

# UNIT TWENTY

## Comprehension A:
1. T    2. F    3. T    4. F    5. F    6. T

## Vocabulary:
1. opportunities, employment    2. antique    3. humiliated    4. froze    5. congregation
6. dropped her off    7. involved

## Cultural Exchange:
1. T    2. T    3. F    4. F    5. T

## Expansion:

```
M E N N O N I T E I D E N C R E K A U Q
A P V D E B K S U E F B H N U I L S N J
E I O T S A T I P H D K I A N C N E I O
W S G S H C T D C L M C G R L S I V T O
F C K I E A O R H X N J E D F N E A L
H O B T J I Q H I N D U F H O J Y N R X
S P C P T C A T H O L I C T R E G T I O
I A O B T M E O B A E B U D H I H A D
W L L B G N O M R P C V Q L Y O J D N O
E I G P R E S B Y T E R I A N V L A U H
J A C E E I L I S N Q H S I M A M Y Q T
P N Z N T M E H A P O O V R D H I A J R
F B P T G H M O R H C M E G P S H D F O
J I K E R E X E K I S G H Y I W B V G N
N A O C B C R W H T M B Q E F I G E O A
O H D O P M H O A Q F D Y Z M T N H I
M A R S K C C A X F P K C Z E N J T H S
R B S T J Q A M G H V J A D L E B I K U
O M V A K F I N I Z Z A B D K S O S A U
M T D L B R A C D B U D D H I S T T R R
```